THE CALLING

An inspirational writing to help believers find their calling from the Lord.

ROBIN GODFREY

THE CALLING

Printed in the United States of America

ISBN-13:978-0692548554
ISBN-10:0692548556

Printed by Createspace 2015
Published by BlaqRayn Publishing Plus 2015

THE CALLING

An inspirational writing to help believers find their calling from the Lord. Ten motivational chapters to propel all to walk in the calling on their life. Loaded with scripture text taken from the King James Version of the Holy Bible, several sermons by Minister Bunkem and discussion questions for individual and group studies.

CONTENTS

The Calling

Introduction:

Each day as humanity rises from sleep, creation wrestles, yet again, with purpose of life uncertainty. As this fact continues to plague the reality of intelligent beings, the world continues its ebb and flow of movement from one day into the next. Most go through life and never invest earnestly in seeking resolution to that inner quest for understanding the human purpose of existing and most importantly, that personal purpose for living.

The pages that follow will give mankind an on-going pulse which leads those who would dare to take a moment in time to do more than simply ponder the questions surrounding purpose. They will lead us to seek real answers to humanity's questions, and those who will seek shall find that which we all need ... resolution.

This book is a compilation of sermons, inspirational writings, quick facts and christian thoughts to inspire believers. It is a challenge for you to discover who it is that you were created to become. If you have already met the challenge of discovery, then you will be inspired to walk in your calling and never look back. Find the chapters that address your quest today and never stop reading until you have reached resolution. You see, when you reach resolution, then and only then will you realize your calling and begin to fulfill your purpose.

Dedication:

Every word is dedicated to my Lord and Savior, Jesus. This book is also dedicated to every man, woman, boy and girl who is saved and still hungry or unsaved and will become saved.

Chapter 9 is dedicated to the survivors of the tragedy at Emanuel AME Church, Charleston, South Carolina, June 17, 2015.

Something is Calling Me to Get Back in the Saddle Again

CHAPTER 1

This Saturday morning, as I picked up pad, paper and Bible and began to organize my thoughts, the very first thing the Lord placed before me was a sermon I had written and delivered more than two years ago. The sermon was entitled, "Something is Calling Me to Get Back in the Saddle Again". It was taken from 1 Samuel 16:7-13, the story of the calling and anointing of David by Samuel. I recognized immediately that the pad I chose was not selected by chance , when I saw that it housed that particular sermon. The title allowed the Lord to use His Word to speak to me at that very moment, as confirmation. I felt Him say, "Yes, my child, I got you up early today, because it is time for you to "Get Back in the Saddle Again". Everything that you have gone through for the past seven years since you answered when I called you to the preaching ministry was done to press you toward and through My purpose for your life. I not only told you to preach. I told you those many years ago to write for Me, speak for Me, inspire My people for Me. And you told Me, Lord, if You allow me to hear You clearly, I will say what You tell me to say, go where You lead me and do what You tell me to do. You felt like you were taken out of the saddle as you preached My Word from church to church, from house to house, on your job, in the grocery store, during Sunday School and Bible Study, during church meetings and even at home. You felt like you were knocked completely out of the saddle as I allowed you to weather the many storms of rejection, ridicule, and judgment. You accepted rejection from some you thought would be there for you to help lead you into obedience to your calling. Many knocked you off of "their" saddle, and I allowed it because I didn't tell you to get in their saddle. However, you were never out of My reach. Today, it's time for you to get back on firm footing. Write what I give you and proclaim My Word through books and letters, speeches and sermons. Write it down again, my child! Write it down and let it live on in all who want to know the truth!" That morning, I reached resolution. We all quest for resolution of purpose. Fact number one is that it only comes when the soul recognizes and knows that it has heard from God.

Yesterday, when the confirmation was given, I didn't even own a computer. I had purchased a total of three in the past seven years, but not one for me. The fourth computer and printer has now been purchased, this time for me, and it is all because He confirmed that it was time to Get Back in the Saddle Again.

Please read the sermon as often as you need it and never stop getting Back in the Saddle Again.

Something is Calling Me to Get Back in the Saddle Again

1 Samuel 16:7-13 (KJV)

7 But the Lord said unto Samuel, Look not on his countenance, or on the height of his stature; because I have refused him: for the Lord seeth not as man seeth; for man looketh on the outward appearance, but the Lord looketh on the heart.

8 Then Jesse called Abinadab, and made him pass before Samuel. And he said, Neither hath the Lord chosen this.

9 Then Jesse made Shammah to pass by. And he said, Neither hath the Lord chosen this.

10 Again, Jesse made seven of his sons to pass before Samuel. And Samuel said unto Jesse, The Lord hath not chosen these.

11 And Samuel said unto Jesse, Are here all thy children? And he said, There remaineth yet the youngest, and, behold, he keepeth the sheep. And Samuel said unto Jesse, Send and fetch him: for we will not sit down till he come hither.

12 And he sent, and brought him in. Now he was ruddy, and withal of a beautiful countenance, and

goodly to look to. And the Lord said, Arise, anoint him: for this is he.

13 Then Samuel took the horn of oil, and anointed him in the midst of his brethren: and the Spirit of the Lord came upon David from that day forward. So Samuel rose up, and went to Ramah.

Have you ever wondered why you are going through so many challenges in life? Most people wonder about life's challenges from time to time. We often wonder what we have done that may have caused what we are going through. Sometimes we wonder how long it will last or if we will survive our struggles. Often times we are lead to believe, much as those in the Old Testament, that challenges, struggles and disappointments are signs that we are living outside of the will of God. This leads us to believe that if we could just change the way we live our lives we will escape many of life's struggles. If we ask each other why bad things happen to good people, the answers would be as many as the number of people we ask. Our time would be better spent pondering what message the Lord is trying to get through to us through our struggles. I believe that we will grow in faith if we direct our search in this area. The great thing is that we can find all of the answers we seek right in the Word.

THE CALLING

Many years ago, I began to watch the westerns on TV on Saturdays. I begin the day looking at the morning news, but I can't wait until 12 noon when the westerns begin. There is one in particular that begins with the cowboy riding up on his big stallion. What I am drawn to is the fact that it doesn't matter what adversity the star of the show faces, it ends with this cowboy again mounting his big stallion and riding off through the dust, and all is well in the world. It doesn't matter if there have been numerous gun fights in the local saloon, shots fired from behind an over-turned barrel, or the famous dual in which the two challengers stand back-to-back and count off three paces, turn and fire. At the end of the show, that cowboy mounts his waiting stallion and rides off in the dust, so that I can watch my westerns again next week. No matter what, the cowboy gets back in the saddle again. This was what came to mind when God gave me this word. The concept of this message is that when a child of God is established in Christ, he will always get back in the saddle again.

So let us examine the scriptures today. We find in 1 Samuel, the anointing of David by Samuel. David, one who was established in the Lord, had no idea that he was chosen by God for His service, as he worked as a shepherd out in the field. We know that David was the author of one of the most well known scriptures in the Bible, Psalm 23. David proclaims in verse 1, ***The Lord is my shepherd; I shall not want***. This verse declares that at the time of this writing, David was firmly convinced that his life was established in the Lord. How many of us are truly able to declare that the Lord is our shepherd? Is He really your shepherd today? Is He still fighting daily to shepherd your life? You see, David knew what it was to be a shepherd, because he was one. But how did he come to the conclusion that the Lord was ***his*** shepherd. Let's revisit what happened when he was chosen.

This would be an ideal place to bring attention to a verse that was not included in the message for today. Verse 1 of this chapter identifies that the Lord chose David, not Samuel. Part B of verse 1 is where the Lord says to Samuel ***fill thine horn with oil, and go, I will send thee to Jesse the Bethlehemite: for I have provided me a king among his sons.*** Samuel was a prophet of the Lord. This meant that he only did what he was sent to do and only had power to anoint someone as it was given to him by God. Otherwise, David would be proclaiming in Psalm 23 that Samuel was his shepherd. Please note that before any man can truly proclaim that the Lord is his shepherd, one must first identify who one's Lord and Master really is. Verse 12 goes on to say, ***And the Lord said, Arise, anoint him: for this is he.*** David was chosen by the Lord and anointed by the Lord. The prophet, Samuel, was chosen as the obedient vessel for the Lord's service. What an awesome blessing it is to be chosen by the Lord, found to be that vessel who not only hears clearly the command of God, but one who God can trust to continue to listen as He leads you on this journey. David understood that he was chosen and anointed by the Lord, as verse 13 says that when Samuel anointed David, in the presence of his brethren, the Spirit of the Lord came upon David from that day forward. Surely, David could loudly proclaim that the Lord is my shepherd, I shall not want.

1 Samuel 16: 7, picks up with one of seven of David's brothers who were ushered before Samuel when he was sent to anoint the future king who was chosen by the Lord. In fact, verse 10 says that his brothers were passed before the prophet twice. We note that David was not even considered by man, not even by his own father, Jesse. David initially wasn't called in to pass before Samuel for consideration at all.

Verse 7 futher explains that the older brothers were passed before the prophet because of their countenance and even height, things that may be impressive to man. But the Lord said to Samuel, ***Look not on his countenance, or on the height of his stature; because I have refused him: for the Lord seeth not as man seeth; for man looketh on***

***the outward appearance, but the Lord looketh on the heart*.**

Our God is the one who will not only choose us, but He is the one who says in His word that He will establish us. He will shepherd us as we step forward in obedience to His calling for our lives.

1 Peter 5:10 says ***But the God of all grace, who hath called us unto his eternal glory by Christ Jesus, after that ye have suffered a while, make you perfect, stablish, strengthen, settle you.*** Are you established in the Lord today? Is He really leading and guiding the decisions in your life? Is He continually perfecting you and strengthening you through life's experiences, with Him in charge of your life? I ask these questions because if the answers are yes, then no matter what life deals you, a child of the Most High God, there will always be Someone (on the inside) calling you to "get back in the saddle again."

2 Peter 1:12 ***Wherefore I will not be negligent to put you always in remembrance of these things, though ye know them, and be established in the present truth.*** In this verse, Paul is preparing his followers for his pending departure. We are not always promised to have someone here available to bring what we should already know back to our remembrance, but if we are established in the fundamentals of salvation [who is our Lord, who is our Savior, who is our Way Maker, who is in control of our down setting and up rising daily, who is it

that decides if we get up or down, move forward or just stand still]... the fundamental truths of a child of God, we have Someone (on the inside) calling us to "get back in the saddle again."

1 Samuel 16:13 again, says that the Spirit of the Lord came upon David from that day forward. Today, we must all come to that day when we accept Jesus as our Lord and Savior, by believing that He is the Messiah who died and paid our sin debt in full and that God, the father, raised Jesus from the dead and if we would confess this truth with our mouth, the Word says, thou shalt be saved. Romans 10:9 says it this way, ***That if thou shalt confess with thy mouth the Lord Jesus, and shalt believe in thine heart that God hath raised him from the dead, thou shalt be saved.*** From that time the Spirit of the Lord does not just come upon us, but comes to dwell inside of us. And that Someone (on the inside) that keeps calling a believer to get back in the saddle again, He is the Holy Spirit, the Spirit of the Living God.

David knew that through countless situations he was to depend on God. He was victorious in the battle with Goliath ***1 Samuel 17:12-54***, and chased by Saul ***1 Samuel 26.*** He was an adulterer ***2 Samuel 11:1-5***, and even a murderer ***2 Samuel 11:14-17.*** But David was also appointed king, he was anointed and he had the Spirit of God upon him. Because his life was firmly in God's hand, as proven time and time again, he could get back in the saddle over and over again.

THE CALLING

In closing, it is easy to simply say, get back in the saddle, but I would not leave you without a few tools to do so. When life has knocked you off of firm footing, sometimes it really is an attack of the enemy, but don't forget that sometimes it is the Lord trying to press us for growth, prepare us for greater service, give us some real life experiences that may be used for His glory.

Stay in the Word

Stay on your knees

Encourage yourself in the Lord

Reflect on what you already know in the Lord

Boldly speak the Word over your own life and situation

Focus on God during adversity

These things may take a day or even weeks, but listen very intently for that still small voice, because Someone will "always" be calling you to "Get Back in the Saddle Again."

As we go forward with self examination and Word examination in our quest to find and fulfill the calling on our lives throughout this book, let us take from the sermon the reminder that first, we must be saved and filled with the Holy Spirit. Then we must continue in development of our relationship with God, so that we hear when He is leading us into service.

The words minister and ministry are widely over-used in the 21st century. We have even come to the point that we call simple acts of kindness, respect and human decency, ministry. Ministry is a word that is used so often that it has become difficult for many people to determine what it is that God has called them to do for the kingdom. If a man opens car doors for women or elderly people, we once thought of this as showing respect. Now, many refer to these acts as services of the Parking Lot Ministry. I brought this out as preamble to asking today, what is the calling on your life? And who has called you? Often times we are so busy doing everything that man has called us to do that we are unable to hear what God is calling us to do. True ministry must not be defined by what someone else says one ought to do or be. True ministry must be defined as service God had ordained a believer to render, for His glory.

David was busy, when he was called in from work to pass before the prophet. I reference this fact to say, the point above is not for us to sit down and stop working in order to find out what our calling is. We must continue to be of service in our local churches. We must, however, be wise enough to understand that we have to learn to recognize the voice of God as opposed to the voice of man. Organized religion has moved in the direction of ministry appointment by man, even if not by God. Samuel was a prophet of the Lord. His title of Prophet did not give him authority to choose David nor power to anoint David. Prophet is more than just a title. It refers to the ministry (service) of the servant.

Acts 17:11 says, ***These were more noble than those in Thessalonica, in that they received the word with all readiness of mind, and searched the scriptures daily, whether those things were so.*** In the preceding sermon, we are challenged to find what our calling is from God. We are encouraged to stay in the Word of God for our answers and directions. We must become as the believers in Berea, who are referenced in this passage of scripture and receive the Word with readiness of mind, that is a determination to act on the Word. And search the scriptures daily, as this is where we find our purpose and strength to stay on course in the midst of a society where there is no lack of people to tell us what to do.

Even though we are amid a society in which it appears we have ministry fraternities, or groups that have come together to choose who they want, who they will support, who they will help in ministry, based upon who will support the group's practices and submit to their authority, the Word also tells us that He has sent pastors after his own heart who will lead us in His service. Please highlight Romans 13 in your bible and pray that God will hide it within your heart today. Verses 1 and 2 says, ***Let every soul be subject unto the higher powers. For there is no power but of God: the powers that be are ordained of God. Whosoever therefore resisteth the power, resisteth the ordinance of God: and they that resist shall receive to themselves damnation.*** We must be sure that we are serving under leaders who are convicted of the Holy Spirit to align with the Word of God and have not become so tainted by the sins of this world that they have sold out on the calling to serve God and not man. Samuel was called, appointed and anointed by God for the work and he served faithfully. As we continually seek the calling on our lives, we need Pastors, Prophets, Preachers and teachers who lead according to that which is given to them from God.

Be encouraged today as you seek the will of God for your life. Speak with your Pastor or leader, whom God has placed over your life. They will be able to help you, as service to the Lord. And don't forget to pray for your leader, because just as the blessing came upon David, through the prophet Samuel, so will your blessing increase through the leader placed over your life. Psalm 133 says, ***Behold, how good and how pleasant it is for brethren to dwell together in unity! It is like the precious ointment upon the head, that ran down upon the beard, even Aaron's beard: that went down to the skirts of his garments; As the dew of Hermon, and as the dew that descended upon the mountains of Zion: for there the Lord commanded the blessing, even life for evermore.***

Submit yourself first, unto God, then unto the leader He has placed over your life. Seek and find what God has really called you to do and to be and you will hear Him, because "Something (Someone) is Calling You to Get Back in the Saddle Again".

FOR DISCUSSION

Chapter 1

1. Did you catch the message of salvation in the sermon?

2. Have you ever felt that you have moved out of sinc with the Lord? If so, did you readily know how to get back on track?

3. Do you feel you have the tools to lead someone to Christ?

4. Have you ever felt pressure to conform to someone else's view of your calling?

5. Do you have a good relationship with someone God has placed over you to help in your spiritual development? Are you willing to take the steps necessary to strengthen that relationship, realizing that God intends that we seek spiritual help from those he has placed over us?

6. What words of encouragement did you feel ministering to you through what you read?

7. How can you help someone else who has become disillusioned in ministry?

8. Do you know what God has called you to do for the Kingdom?

9. Are you motivated to equip yourself for the mission you are called to fulfill?

10. Are you ready to face the areas of weakness and challenge in your life that may be affecting how motivated you are to obey God?

Are You Ready to Generate Something For the Lord?

CHAPTER 2

There is saying that was once very popular in America. So much so that we found on many bumper stickers these four letters WWJD to represent the saying, What would Jesus do. In fact, I preached a sermon that included that saying some time ago. But that is not what we are leading into today. Instead, it is required that we examine our creation in this chapter, as we are further motivated to be who we are in Christ. We refer to the saying though for us to think about how we make decisions daily. Do we pause throughout the day to think about what Jesus would have us to do or say when we choose how to proceed? And do we really think that simply taking that momentary pause is enough to assure that we are making the right choices? I don't think so. It is a good way for us not to rush into things or a good reminder that we are not to make decisions on our own, but the Word teaches us to spend more than just momentary pauses before we leap. I encourage you to look again at WWJD and see it as more than just an idea about pausing throughout the day, but see it as a great thought to remind us to get in the Word of God, so that throughout our lives we know what Jesus would have us to do.

Each day, we are sprinkled out, as out of a salt shaker, and told to season this world. You may be familiar with that scripture. But everywhere we go we find people who don't believe as we do. We find people and more people and for every person in our lives we find differences of opinions and differences of levels of understanding. These factors are what make us individuals. While posing countless challenges for us to be who we are, our differences also serve to make us interesting. Our differences make life exciting as each day is different from the one before it. Some times we begin the day with a well planned goal in mind; it could be something as simple as "I am going to get my house cleaned before head hits pillow tonight."

And somewhere along the way, we end up going to the store because we got a call from Mother, or just going to answer the door, we end up on the front porch in conversation with a neighbor. But whatever may happen, we find time running out on getting the house cleaned before the day ends. In much the same way, we begin days with the intent to season this world and as we encounter different people we are faced with conversations going in different directions than we intended as people are unique in their level of intellect, understanding, beliefs, etc. So as one day goes into another, we ask ourselves if we are accomplishing what we have been sent out to do.

For the Christian, we sometimes become overwhelmed with all we have been called to do, when much time passes and it doesn't appear that we are getting the job done. Most recently, I found myself in prayer asking the Lord to restore His joy to me. I asked that He renew my Spirit and revive my soul. I found myself longing for times in my past during which I was "on fire" for the things of God. Oh yes, there were definitely times when I couldn't get enough of the Word. I was full of energy. I was focused. I was so excited about Jesus that no one could come near me without feeling my excitement. You may relate to times in your life when you knew that you were walking seasoning for the world. As we mature in our faith walk, we realize that it is not real to think that we are called to operate in a permanent state of "happiness and hunger" for lack of a better description, at all times. We realize that in Christ, we are stabilized to live our lives for Him in such a calm assurance that others will see His good works through us and glorify Him. This reality calls us to the understanding that it doesn't matter who we come in contact with and no matter how our days go through the twists and turns called life, we must equip ourselves to be steadfast and unmovable if we are going to make any headway for the Lord. So I turn our attention to WWJD, that popular saying that would direct us back to His Word.

Does it seem impossible to you today, to run on (doing all the things God has called you to do), while looking at this world that is so full of sin? Are you finding WWJD as helpful in making right choices concerning your area of the world you are called to season? In other words, are you finding yourself drawn to the Word of God for direction, to be renewed, revived, re-filled with His joy? Well, I found in the Word something very helpful and encouraging and the sermon found in this chapter will allow me to share it with you. It is the fact that God never told us to go out there and create anything. In fact, He created everything that you and I will ever need to be able to fulfill His calling on our lives. I thought that it was refreshing and I know that it will renew your life. How could I possible know this? Well, as the preachers always say, I'm so glad you asked that question. The Word says in

Isaiah 55: 10-11, *For as the rain cometh down, and the snow from heaven, and returneth not thither, but watereth the earth, and maketh it bring forth and bud, that it may give seed to the sower, and bread to the eater: So shall my word be that goeth forth out of my mouth; it shall not return unto me void, but it shall accomplish that which I please, and it shall prosper in the thing whereto I sent it.* Hallelujah!

Genesis 1:26-31 (KJV)

26 And God said, Let us make man in our image, after our likeness: and let them have dominion over the fish of the sea, and over the fowl of the air, and over the cattle, and over all the earth, and over every creeping thing that creepeth upon the earth.

27 So God created man in his own image, in the image of God created he him; male and female created he them.

28 And God blessed them, and God said unto them, Be fruitful, and multiply, and replenish the earth, and subdue it: and have dominion over the fish of the sea, and over the fowl of the air, and over every living thing that moveth upon the earth.

29 And God said, Behold, I have given you every herb bearing seed, which is upon the face of all the earth, and every tree, in the

which is the fruit of a tree yielding seed; to
you it shall be for meat.
30 And to every beast of the earth, and to
every fowl of the air, and to every thing
that creepeth upon the earth, wherein
there is life, I have given every green herb
for meat: and it was so.
31 And God saw every thing that he had
made, and, behold, it was very good. And
the evening and the morning were the
sixth day.

Generate
Be Fruitful, Multiply, Replenish

From the Genesis (beginning) of mankind, you were very good, according to the Word of God. It is also true to say that God has never made a mistake. The Word we are learning from today is generally defined as the creation story. From this story we find who created the heavens, the earth, mankind, and every creature that was created. If we examine the text closely, we will also find that God gave us divine order for living our lives in Him. We will focus on His command that we ***Be Fruitful, Multiply and Replenish*** His created work. In order to receive His command for man, we must understand that The Creator knew exactly what He was doing when He created us and everything else that He created. To get this understanding, let us take a moment to look at the order in which the creation took place. We are picking up today on verse 26 of chapter one. We find in this verse that when God says let us make man in our image, after our likeness, He had already created the things that man was to have dominion over, before He created man. The Word says, and let them have dominion over the fish of the sea (created on the fifth day, vs 20), and over the fowl of the air (also created on day 5, vs 21), and over the cattle (vs 22 affirms day #6, which was also the day He created man), and over all the earth (created on the first day, Genesis 1:1), and over every creeping thing that creepeth upon the earth (vs 24, the 6th day). Let's skip down to verse 29 when He says Behold, I have given you every herb bearing seed, which is upon the face of all the earth, and every tree, wherein there is live, I have given every green herb for meat (vs 11-13 says they were created on the 3rd day). So here in this 1st chapter, man finds that God indeed created everything that we would need to live and accomplish what He intended, before He created us. Taking this scripture line by line like this is how we utilize our intellect and our senses to see what The Lord has placed before us.

We began by saying that we needed to understand that God knew what He was doing when He created us in order for us to receive (to act on) His command for us. As we embrace our calling in the 21st century, we must become painfully aware that we have to dig much deeper than our common intellect and our natural God given sense, if we are to act on His commands. Digging much deeper simply refers to getting in the Spirit. With the vision of the Spirit, we take this lesson of creation and understand that we came some time after this creation experience. In fact, we are found after chapter 3 of Genesis, after the fall of man, after sin has entered into the picture. Therefore it is no longer good enough to simply say that God created everything in proper order, as the detailed review of chapter one shows us.

Isn't it good to know that before God ***called*** us to be who He created us to be, He created everything you and I would need to accomplish His will. The statement sounds repetitive, but it really is not. Look a little closer and you will find that this statement refers to after the fall in chapter 3. This statement is also after your salvation and mine. This statement is after we have heard from the Master what His calling is on our lives. The difference indeed is that in Genesis 1, God commanded that man, created perfectly in perfect surroundings, with everything he needed, was to be fruitful, multiply, and replenish His earth, referring to His physical creation. How do we know this? We do not find where God tells man to have dominion over man. After the fall of man, we find that this same God is sending man out with a command to bring man back to Himself (back to chapter 1), back to his creation of perfect order, back to rule over His creation. What an awesome task He has left in your hands and mine! It would seem almost impossible, as we view the task at hand from the vantage point of sin running rampant in the world. It really seems to be impossible to turn this huge ship around and back toward God, when we appear to be too few in number, too weak as an army, too divided as a people. But I was called to challenge any of us who feel defeated today, by the overwhelming task at hand to get in the Spirit! Get in the Spirit and see that there are far too many victories in our history to turn and run in fear today, when we see the calling on our lives to turn man back to God.

Get in the Spirit and find in Genesis 1 that God told everything He created what to do and He tells us what to do as well. We are not alone. We are not out numbered. We are not defeated. In verse 6 God tells the firmament He created to divide the waters and it obeyed. In verse 11 He told the earth to bring forth grass and it obeyed. Verses 16-18 He created two great lights, told light to shine and light shines even now. One shines over day and one over night, and stars shine as well. He commanded them, they obeyed and still obey His will even now. What a victory for our Lord! In verse 22 we find that He blessed waters, and the fowl of the air, and every living creature and told them also to be fruitful and multiply. They have been obedient and His truth is marching on! We still have birds flying in the air and fish in the sea. We have what we need to obey our God and turn this world around for His glory. But in order to walk in the calling on our lives, we must get in His word and get in the Spirit to see that we can obey what He commands of us and we can be victorious in our calling.

Point number 1 is that God knew exactly what He was doing when He created us. Point number 2 is that He created everything that we would need to accomplish His calling on our lives. Now we will deal with the 3rd and final point of this message. Point number 3 is that God called us to generate, not to create. Verse 28 reads, ***And God blessed them, and God said unto them, Be fruitful, and multiply,*** *and replenish the earth, and subdue it: and have dominion over the fish of the sea and over the fowl of the air, and over every living thing that moveth upon the earth.* God had already created it all. Now as we receive (prepare to act on) His command for our lives, let us look at the command in verse 28 from the point of the 21st century, way after the fall of man. God never told us to create anything. He said for us to be fruitful. Let's examine what is meant here for us. In John 15: 1-5 Jesus says,

> **"I am the true vine, and my Father is the husbandman.**
> **Every branch in me that beareth not fruit he taketh away: and every branch that beareth fruit, he purgeth it, that it may bring forth more fruit.**
> **Now ye are clean through the word which I have spoken unto you.**
> **Abide in me, and I in you. As the**

> **branch cannot bear fruit of itself, except it abide in the vine; no more can ye, except ye abide in me.**
> **I am the vine, ye are the branches: He that abideth in me, and I in him, the same bringeth forth much fruit: for without me ye can do nothing.."**

To be fruitful is to be full of fruit (bearing fruit). When we bear (carry) fruit we will also reproduce or make more of what we have inside of us, but there is a stark difference between bearing fruit and reproducing fruit. In the context of the command in Genesis 1, this refers to being full of fruit. We can determine this because if this fruitful referred to reproducing, then we would not have the continued commands of Multiply and Replenish. But instead we can receive that we must first be full of fruit and then can we multiply and replenish. Look at what the word says to us today in

Galatians 5:22-23: ***But the fruit of the Spirit is love, joy, peace, longsuffering, gentleness, goodness, faith, meekness, temperance: against such there is no law.*** Certainly, here we can see that these are the fruit that are produced within the believer, not just what we are to produce in others. But we are to be full of the fruit of the Spirit.

Now the word tells us to multiply (the fruit). This is the call to let the fruit grow by reproduction. This happens as we feed on the Word, as we meditate and commune with God through the Spirit, as we seek His will and listen for His voice. Stop just a moment and remember that He already created and gave to us everything that we would need to fulfill His command on our lives. See again in verse 2 of John 15 where Jesus says that every branch that beareth fruit, he purges it, that it may bring forth more fruit. We are not alone, when he commands that we multiply in fruit.

Part three of His command is that we Replenish the earth. Now this is the part where He is telling us to **generate**, not to create. This is the command that we share the fruit, pass the fruit out within His world. In Genesis He is referring to the continuance of His perfect creation by operating in His intended state for the world he made. Today as we transition into walking in the calling on our individual lives and the calling on our lives within the scope of corporate fellowship as believers, let us seek what His intent for us was from this command to replenish in Genesis 1. Again, I must remind us that I explained earlier that in order for us to glean our Lord's message for the church today, we must "get in the Spirit". So, in the Spirit, we know that God created the whole world and all in it with knowledge of the fall of man, which occurs in chapter 3 of Genesis. We realize that Genesis meaning beginning does not supersede the fact that God is Alpha and Omega, beginning and end, knows all things and knew all things always. When we refer to order, we consider earthly order (that which man can understand and relate to in our flesh) and then there is divine order (spiritual order where there is no real beginning and end, no time as we understand it as those who were created). In spiritual terms, this just means that ***God is the I am that I am.*** In human understanding, He knew what was going to happen before it happened. This also means that He prepared all things for addressing everything that would happen, because He is God. When we look at the command to replenish the earth from the view point of Genesis, within the creation story, we find that God is commanding "first man" to replenish, to care for His creation, to oversee all He created, to nurture and observe and enjoy His creation, and to reproduce what He created. This is for human to make more humans, for fish and fowl to make more fish and fowl, not by creating but by generating more from what He had created.

After the fall of man, we find that God is now sending man after man, prophet after prophet, disciple after disciple to **replenish** the earth. This replenishing now refers to bringing His creation back to Himself, back to it's original purpose of communion with Him, as He created us to be. We find the command for the 21st century repeated in the New Testament in Matthew 28:19-20, ***Go ye therefore and teach all nations, baptizing them in the name of the Father, and of the Son, and of the Holy Ghost: Teaching them to observe all things whatsoever I have commanded you: and, lo, I am with you always, even unto the end of the world. Amen.*** This is the command to replenish the earth. Thus ends the explanation of Point number 3. God called us to generate, not to create.

I proclaim today that God gave us everything we need to obey His command. Even after man fell from perfect communion with God, God gave us what we needed by sending Himself into the world, in the form of a man, Jesus, to die for all of our sins and pay our sin debt in full, thereby providing us that tree by which we may come back to communion with Him. The challenge that each of us face daily is finding out what is it specifically that He has called us to do as individuals. Each of us was not called to preach. Each was not called to prophesy. Each wasn't called to teach. We weren't all called to be a writer. We were not all sent to go out to other countries on the mission field. So what were you called to do? We were all called to be fruitful, multiply and replenish. We were all called to Go ye therefore, as indicated in Matthew. In Genesis, the light was not commanded to swim with the fish and the trees were not told to reproduce the creeping things God created. There is a divine order and a sovereign command on our lives, but as believers we must be willing to read and study the word. We must be determined to get in the Spirit in order to hear what the Word is saying to us today as individuals.

The only way that any man can accomplish what he is intended to do is first to be born again. There is no other way that one could possibly receive and act on their calling without first surrendering their life of flesh and sin to a new life in Christ. The Word teaches us that in order to be born again, we must accept Jesus as Lord for ourselves. Romans 10: 9-10 says, ***That if thou shalt confess with thy mouth the Lord Jesus, and shalt believe in thine heart that God***

hath raised him from the dead, thou shalt be saved. For with the heart man believeth unto righteousness; and with the mouth confession is made unto salvation. It is not good enough to simply quote the scriptures with an understanding born of our intellect. We must put the scriptures into action, so if you are reading this today or hearing it (receiving it in your heart as truth), if indeed this day you know that Jesus is Lord and that that He died for your sins on Calvary's cross and that God raised Jesus from the dead, then pray these words of confession openly.

Father God, please forgive me for every one of my sins. I repent and am sorry. I believe that your son Jesus is Lord. I believe that He died and paid for my sins. I believe that You raised Him from the dead and I receive Him as Lord of my life this day. I trust that I am now saved in accord with Your word and I give you thanks for saving me. Now, Lord, please speak to my heart and lead me in my new walk as a member of Your family. I am willing to do what You lead me to do and I need to hear You. Please lead me and I will follow. In Jesus' name I pray. Amen.

If you prayed that prayer in truth, my brother or my sister, you are now born again. Begin to read the Word of God as a new person, a believer. Pray daily for God to show you the church He would have you to join, so that you may study His Word with others who believe. Pray that He will lead you to a place with the leader through whom He will continue to lead you in His call for your life. It is my prayer that as you receive these words you will reflect on this sermon and know that the commands that God has given us are not too difficult for us to accomplish, as He never told us to do it alone. He didn't tell us to create anything. He commanded that we generate much through what He already created. Once we are saved,

God's Spirit comes to live within us as believers. His Word says,

Be Fruitful (full of fruit), Multiply (increase in fruit through His Word) and Replenish (nurture and develop His creation, bringing others into His body). Hallelujah!

FOR DISCUSSION

Chapter 2

1. Did you get the invitation to salvation from the sermon?
2. Have there been times in your life when you felt overwhelmed by your calling? Did you find words that help you better deal with the stress and challenges you face in being true to your calling?
3. Are you able to lead others who may be faced with the struggles in ministry to strength through God's Word?
4. Have you researched the Bible for words to be used in leading others from a life of sin to safety in God's family?
5. Discuss how many members of the same family are called to operate in different functions in order to accomplish the same mission? If reading this alone, take time to meditate on this factor of diversity.
6. Did you find within the message that

there may be value in finding out what God has called you to do and that by coming to that knowledge it may yield more fruit for your journey?

7. Think about the fruit of the Spirit and search for ways that each fruit serves to equip us for living victorious lives in Christ.

Freedom Isn't Free
CHAPTER 3

23 "When thou sittest to eat with a ruler, consider diligently what is before thee:
2 And put a knife to thy throat, if thou be a man given to appetite.
3 Be not desirous of his dainties: for they are deceitful meat.
4 Labour not to be rich: cease from thine own wisdom.
5 Wilt thou set thine eyes upon that which is not? for riches certainly make themselves wings; they fly away as an eagle toward heaven.
6 Eat thou not the bread of him that hath an evil eye, neither desire thou his dainty meats:
7 For as he thinketh in his heart, so is he: Eat and drink, saith he to thee; but his heart is not with thee.
8 The morsel which thou hast eaten shalt thou vomit up, and lose thy sweet words.
9 Speak not in the ears of a fool: for he will despise the wisdom of thy words..."

We live in a country where we often take for granted our freedom. We feel that we are free to live where we choose, work where we want, and do many of the things that we choose to do. We choose the politicians we will support, the church we will join, the organizations we will commit to, and the shows we will watch. We choose what type of clothes we will wear, the schools we will attend, and so many other things. The many choices we are free to make concerning our lives really lead us to feel that indeed we are free. There are a few days yearly that we pause to acknowledge those in our military who have served in order to allow us these freedoms and so many others. When we think of those who have given their lives and limbs in war, most of us can see that our freedom really isn't free. Much of what we enjoy and sometimes take for granted today was paid for by the sacrifices of others. Much of what our children enjoy has been paid for by the sacrifices that we as parents have made.

The scripture we are focusing on today, reminds us that everything we may receive is not necessarily free. It focuses primarily on eating with one who is in authority and warns us to be aware that what we are partaking of may come with a price. Verse 1 says, ***When thou sittest to eat with a ruler, consider diligently what is before thee***: The second part of that verse which says to consider diligently what is before thee, certainly is not referring to what the food is that is being offered. This is not a suggestion that the food may not be nourishing or appetizing. Indeed, this word is referring to what else is before us in addition to the food. It makes us question the times when we have been offered things that came with strings attached. Have you ever been offered friendship, with strings attached? What about the most common of offerings, like conversation, with strings attached? Oh, we have all spoken to those we feel we have to watch every word we say, because quite simply, the conversation comes with strings attached. I recall hearing adults saying, "Free things will kill you", when I was young. I have found over the years that they knew what they were talking about. There are many things in life that appear to be free, but they really are not. These suggestions don't sound very much like the description of christian behavior or concerns, but we find here in Proverbs, the book of wisdom, that there is this section of warning to be wise concerning who we sit at the table with. If we heed the wisdom of scriptures, we may find that we are giving away so much more than what we are receiving, at the table. Proverbs says "consider diligently". This suggests that a wise person would not ignore that gut feeling that something isn't quite right here.

Verse 2 goes on to address those who need to be extra careful, because they have a good appetite. It suggests that one puts a knife to his throat if he is lead by his appetite. I don't think this is suggesting suicide, but just ensuring that we aren't out there so hungry that we can't use some common sense. Let us take this lesson away from the literal table of food. The warning extends to the believer not getting so carried away in the good time we are having that we disconnect from the Spirit on the inside, warning us to be careful. Proverbs is telling the wise to even reject that which is not offered with a "right" spirit, but instead is offered with manipulative intent (see verse 3) ***Be not desirous of his dainties: for they are deceitful meat.***

Verse 4 is transitional, stating ***Labour not to be rich:***

cease from thine own wisdom. This verse more firmly begins to address our heart, our reason for sitting at the table. It is so much easier for us to read this scripture and address the ruler's deceitful heart, but it is so much more fruitful for us to reference the Word which also tells us in ***Jeremiah 17:9 The heart is deceitful above all things, and desperately wicked: who can know it?*** Jeremiah is not simply referring to the heart of rulers. He is referring to any heart that is not being ruled by the Spirit of God. So in this Proverb, by Solomon, we find a greater focus on the heart of the one who is committing himself to join in this offering from the ruler. What is our intent when we sit or partake or join in the big fun, with someone who does not have a "right" spirit or a "right" intent toward the things of God? Where are we coming from when we choose to join in when we know, through the Spirit that indwells us, that there indeed are strings attached? Well, if we go on to the next verse, I believe that Solomon is suggesting that sometimes its more than just that we have a great appetite as mentioned in verse 2. Certainly, we must admit that sometimes it is just that we want to be "in the know". I have been known to call this nosiness having a diagnosis of the Need to Knows. Those who are closest to me know that I have been saying for many years that the person who invents the pill to suppress or control man's Need to Know disease will be rich, because sometimes we put our spiritual selves at risk simply because we just have to know all of the goings on first. In verse 4, the Word is saying it's still a little more than that. Indeed, we find with a little self examination that we place ourselves at the table because we are trying to get something ourselves. Verse 4 says simply, don't work so hard to get what we desire and stop relying our our own wisdom (that's the wisdom of the flesh) to gain riches. So now the question posed to the believer is, What is it that we want so badly, what riches are worth putting our spiritual health at stake in order to obtain it? I will pick up on this point in a moment, but it is necessary to temper this with a little seasoning, as the Word advises us to do, so let's go somewhere else for a little diversion.

The Word teaches us that the enemy comes in to kill, so let's address this right now. ***John 10:10 The thief cometh not, but for to seal, and to kill, and to destroy: I am come that they might have life, and that they might have it more abundantly.*** I make this reference at this time because whenever we are called to check ourselves and our own motives, Satan steps in to tell us that the one delivering the message is picking on us. This is where we begin to shut down and start asking the questions, Who does he/she think they are to start digging into my motives as if they have it all together? and so forth. As believers, we have to be willing to get in the Spirit of this Word in order to receive the deeper meaning of the Word of God for us today. Yes, the Word is "for us" today. This means for our development in Christ, for our use for the victory He has already ordained for our lives. This means it is not sent forth to beat us down, but instead to build up the body of Christ for greater works. Therefore, as we go back where we left off in dealing with ourselves, we need to go back into it together. What we have to understand is that before the Word comes forth with power "to accomplish that for which it was sent", it is given to the preacher "to convict the preacher first". Therefore it comes with Power and Conviction. I look at self first and say, why have I sat at the deceiving table? Why have taken of the sweet treats offered? What is it that I want to gain so badly that I have been willing to put my own soul at risk to obtain it? This is not a Word for you only, this is a Word for self first. So we determine to put Satan under our feet! We step on the devil's head as we return to this self examination Word.

Again verse 4 is a warning that we, in our flesh, our willing to work too hard to try to gain what we "think" we want. He is saying, stop putting ourselves at risk going after what God already said He will give to the heart that is right. So keep our hearts right, our intentions righteous. How can we do this in light of the Word also warning us that the heart is deceitful? Hint: He never told us to act on our heart, but move by His Spirit.

Verse 5 goes on to say that we are not to set our eyes on that which is not, because what we gain by doing so will take wings and fly away, just like an eagle flies toward heaven. This means that none of us can change the will of God for our lives, by going after that which is not the intent of God for us. In other words, only what we do for God will last. Proverbs 10:2 says ***Treasure of wickedness***

profit nothing: but righteousness delivereth from death. Matthew 16:26 says ***For what is a man profited, if he should gain the whole world and lose his own soul? Or what shall a man give in exchange for his soul?*** Again the question is what is it we are after when we are willing to place our spiritual health at risk? The truth is found in ***Matthew 6:33 But seek ye first the kingdom of God, and his righteousness; and all these things shall be added unto you.*** And verse 27 of the same says ***Which of you by taking thought can add one cubit unto his stature?***

Today let's refocus on the message within the message, freedom isn't really free. We spoke earlier about the fact that many who served in our military had to give up life and limb that we might enjoy the level of freedom we now enjoy. Many parents had to give up much in order for children to enjoy the things in life they have. What must we give up to live a life of freedom in Christ? Well we reference that appetite for things that God never intended for us to have. This could be a title, a position, more wealth, that house with the two car garage. None of these things are bad for us to desire nor are any of them things that God may not choose for us to have as His followers. The point is are we willing to lose our very souls to obtain them. The Word says ***Matthew 23:11-12 But he that is greatest among you shall be your servant. And whosoever shall exalt himself shall be abased; and he that shall humble himself shall be exalted.*** And He says in 1 Peter 5:6 ***Humble yourselves therefore under the mighty hand of God, that he***

may exalt you in due time: We see that when we are willing to yield ourselves to the Spirit of God, we find that His yoke is easy and His burdens are light. It is easier and lighter to walk in what God has prepared for us to walk in than it is to seek after what we want for ourselves. Oh He also says that He will give us the desires of our heart. But these verses in Proverbs 23 are a warning that what we seek after, that is not within the will of our Lord for us, will fly away.

Let us complete our study of these verses for now. Verses 6-8 goes on to tell us what to do. Solomon says do not eat the bread of him that hath an evil eye, and do not desire his dainty meats. It says as he thinks in his heart, so is he. He summons us to eat and drink, but his heart is not with us. Therefore, what we eat we shall vomit up and lose our sweet words. This means that because first our own heart isn't right and our own intentions are not really pure, plus the one who is serving the dish is just as deceitful as we are, we are going to find ourselves sick. This is soul sickness, not physical sickness. When we invite this type of devilment into our lives as believers, all we can possibly take in is wickedness. Then what we have on the inside is what we begin to vomit out. Don't take these verses lightly, for in them we find out just how we give ourselves over to the enemy for his use. Now we are going about in this world spreading no good thing. Why, because instead of walking in obedience to God, we have placed our spiritual health in the hands of the enemy. What I want us to get today is that we give up our freedom to walk with our Lord, hearing clearly what He is commanding us to do and be in this world, when we put our communion with Him at risk to get what we "think" we want. Now we are expecting a clean, pure, holy God to dwell in an unclean place and use us for His glory. I suggest to the body today, than when this becomes our manner of attaining our goals, we are first not much good for ourselves and certainly we are not of much good for the Master. Again, freedom isn't free. If we want to walk in God's victory we have got to be willing to give up this worldly, fleshly appetite for gaining what is not ours to gain and knowing every little detail He never intended for us to know.

The final verse reads ***Speak not in the ears of a fool: for he will despise the wisdom of thy words.***
Let us say that this is not a word for fools, but a word for those who want to walk in communion with our Lord. It is not a word that leads believers to walk through life suspicious of every act of kindness or every offer of true friendship. This is a word that leads us to lean and depend on the Spirit of God, which is on the inside of us and not on man's words. It's for those who desire the pure milk of the Word of God, because we want to live for Him, to serve Him, to win souls for Him, and to bring glory to His name. See, at the table of deceit, we begin to give out to the adversary the pearls of wisdom which only comes to those who come before God in Spirit and in truth. And this Word says that he will despise the wisdom of our words. See ***Matthew 7:6*** says ***Give not that which is holy unto the dogs, neither cast ye your***

pearls before swine, lest they trample them under their feet, and turn again and rend you. Let's take the warnings seriously. Not only will the one we have placed our trust in despise our wisdom, but he will also step on the Word of God and turn and tear us up and down for thinking that by communion with God we can really hear from Him and think that we know something. So now this describes that we are not only going out into the world with nothing but what we took into ourselves at the table of deceit, but we are also beat down by the one we sat with, plus we are no longer of service for our Lord to bring Him glory. On top of all of this, what we were seeking after, we may have gained (power, title, position, wealth, acceptance), but Proverbs says it's all for nothing, because it will fly away and Matthew says what profit is it if we gain all of these things and lose our very soul.

But I paused in this Word, and I found strength for the journey today. I found that freedom to live for Christ isn't free. We have got to give up those things that are not of Christ to move forward gaining the blessings of Christ. We are reminded in this lesson that salvation is now free, not because there wasn't a cost to be paid ***For the wages of sin is death; but the gift of God is eternal life through Christ Jesus our Lord*** according to Romans 6:23. Oh yes, we do not have to walk in darkness on this side and then transition on to eternal death, and it is because Jesus came into this world, more than 2000 years ago. He walked in a way that showed us how to walk the walk. But He also came to pay the penalty for your sin and mine. So they hung Him on Calvary's cross and He became sin who knew no sin in order to free those who were sinners so that they may come back to the Father. He paid the cost, because freedom isn't free. He died a real death and descended into hell for our sins. But God, the Father, raised Him up on the third day and He is now on the right hand of the Father making intercession for us. That's why eternal life is described as a gift. The Word teaches us that if we believe in our hearts that Jesus is Lord and if we would confess this with our mouth, we shall be saved.

When we are saved, we no longer have to live in bondage to any man. In salvation we pass from death into life and it is a life of true freedom. We turn away from the table of any man who has a heart of deceit, realizing that freedom isn't free. To walk in this freedom, we have to give up the Need to Knows, the self elevation methods, the offers waived in our faces that we will be somebody if we take on relationships with those who can exalt us. Get in the Word and get in the Spirit and find these words in ***John 8:32 And ye shall know the truth, and the truth shall make you free.*** And this confirmation in ***John 8:36 If the Son therefore shall make you free, ye shall be free indeed.***

If you believe that Jesus is Lord and that God raised Him from the dead then confess it openly with your mouth and the Word says, thou shalt be saved. ***Hallelujah!***

///

When I began this work it was not my intent that every chapter would include a sermon, nevertheless, not my will but Thine be done. I find that it is imperative, if we are to walk in our calling, that we must be armed with the ***sword of the Spirit, which is the Word of God. Ephesians 6:17 part B.*** Whenever a child of God steps out with determination to be obedient to Him, we are faced with the fiery darts of the enemy. It is too often that we seem to go forward in a cloud of happiness with great ideas that we are all in this together. Sometimes we begin to place our trust in man instead of in the One who was called out of darkness to walk in His marvelous light. We must be mindful that the enemy sends those darts in many packages. Sometimes the attacks come from outside of the body of Christ and there are times they come from within the body. But we have not been left defenseless because we have the Word of God.

It is my hope that we find within His Word that there is no attack against us personally, but instead, there is knowledge, wisdom and understanding for us to run on and see what the end is going to be. ***John 3:17*** says ***For God sent not his Son into the world to condemn the world; but that the world through him might be saved.*** Also we find in Romans ***8:1 There is therefore now no condemnation to them which are in Christ Jesus, who walk not after the flesh, but after the Spirit.*** Be encouraged today. If after reading this chapter, you find that you are feeling condemned or defeated, I speak into your Spirit right now that, that feeling is not coming from The Lord. That is simply an attack from our enemy who seeks to tear down the things of God. So I end this short chapter with these encouraging words found in ***Psalm 24:7-10 Lift up your heads, O ye gates; and be ye lift up, ye everlasting doors; and the King of glory shall come in. Who is this King of glory? The Lord strong and mighty, the Lord mighty in battle. Lift up your heads, O ye gates; even lift them up, ye everlasting doors; and the King of glory shall come in. Who is this King of glory? The Lord of hosts, he is the King of glory. Selah.***

He came to remind us to be thankful for the sacrifices that have been made by our military, our parents, those in our churches who came before we did, and those saints in the Bible who serve us even now. Be thankful for every member of the body who offer true friendship and true relationships with us for the battle ahead. Most of all, be thankful that Jesus paid the ultimate price for our freedom as we choose to walk with Him and for Him in true liberty. And we thank Him now for opening our eyes through Proverbs 23:1-9 to not only see the description of others who may be walking in error, but also to see His message for us today as we seek to follow Him.

FOR DISCUSSION

Chapter 3

1. Are you better able to recognize the devise of the enemy from review of this Word?
2. Are you able to warn others, with a Spirit of meekness and humility, when you perceive that they may be walking in error?
3. Did you find that invitation to salvation within the message?
4. Discuss the chastisement of the Word and how it does not come to the believers with condemnation. If you are reading this alone, take a moment to think on the difference between chastisement (correction) and condemnation.
5. Did the Word lead you into self examination, as opposed to judgment of others?

Chapter 4

What is Offered At the Table of Our Lord

There are so many great characteristics of God that we never stop learning more and more about Him. One of them is that He is the God who finishes everything that He begins. ***Philippians 1:6*** says, ***Being confident of this very thing, that he which hath begun a good work in you will perform it until the day of Jesus Christ:*** and ***John 19:30*** states, ***When Jesus therefore had received the vinegar, he said,*** It is Finished: ***and he bowed his head, and gave up the ghost.*** Another characteristic found in the Word concerning Jesus is found in ***Exodus 34:14*** which states, ***For thou shalt worship no other god: for the Lord, whose name is Jealous, is a jealous God:*** Well quite a while after completing the third chapter, in which we did a study from Proverbs concerning sitting at the table of rulers who have no positive intent, the Lord dropped in my Spirit the fact that we didn't look at what is found at the table prepared by the Lord. So we had a little talk about what He would have me to share on that topic. I waited for a Word from Him for myself and for you. I thought about the story in which He sent for the gentiles to be invited into share in a feast, because the chosen people rejected Him and many other stories in the Bible, but He did not confirm any of them. Instead, He let me know that He had already given me a sermon, which you are about to read. He had me to review it and see that He multiplied food and fed many. Why would we feel the need to go to anyone else to be fed. As you share in this message, you will find that it has much more intent than the filling of physical food. Our Lord offers us everything that we will ever need to fulfill

His call on our lives.

Matthew 4:3-4 says, ***And when the tempter came to him, he said, If thou be the Son of God, command that these stones be made bread. But he answered and said, It is written, Man shall not live by bread alone, but by every word that proceedeth out of the mouth of God.*** What a word! I don't think that by reading the Word to come you will find yourself hungry for bread and fish, but you will find yourself hungry for souls. Our Lord offers us so much more than things to satisfy our flesh. He satisfies us with Himself. Every day that we grow in our walk with Him, He responds to our faith with revealing more and more of Himself to us. So I will ask a few questions before you go into the Word. Are you eager to be more effective in ministry? Do you desire to make a change in your family, in your church or maybe within your community? Do you want to see this world changed *because God used you to make the changes? Well, I believe that if you are able to receive the message of* ***Luke 9:10-17****, (and remember to receive it is to act on it), you will go out into your calling and go out into this world, with purpose of mind to make changes for The Lord.*

These Feet Were Made for Holiness

10 "And the apostles, when they were returned, told him all that they had done. And he took them, and went aside privately into a desert place belonging to the city called Bethsaida.

11 And the people, when they knew it, followed him: and he received them, and spake unto them of the kingdom of God, and healed them that had need of healing.

12 And when the day began to wear away, then came the twelve, and said unto him, Send the multitude away, that they may go into the towns and country round about, and lodge, and get victuals: for we are here in a desert place.

13 But he said unto them, Give ye them to eat. And they said, We have no more but five loaves and two fishes; except we should go and buy meat for all this people.

14 For they were about five thousand men. And he said to his disciples, Make them sit down by fifties in a company.

15 And they did so, and made them all sit down.

16 Then he took the five loaves and the two fishes, and looking up to heaven, he blessed them, and brake, and gave to the disciples to set before the multitude.

17 And they did eat, and were all filled: and there was taken up of fragments that remained to them twelve baskets.

18 And it came to pass, as he was alone praying, his disciples were with him: and he asked them, saying, Whom say the people that I am?

19 They answering said, John the Baptist; but some say, Elias; and others say, that one of the old prophets is risen again.."

Focus Verse: Luke 9:13 (NIV)

He replied, "You give them something to eat." They answered, "We have only five loaves of bread and two fish—unless we go and buy food for all this crowd."

HISTORY

Just before this well know scripture lesson, in which Jesus is known to have fed the five thousand, not counting women and children, He had performed several miracles while the disciples were with Him. They are listed below.

Luke 8: 22-25 is the account of Jesus and the disciples in the ship, when the storm began to rage. They came running to Him to ask if He were going to allow them to drown. As the song goes, "that's when Jesus got up, in the middle of the boat and said, O peace be still." But the question He asked the disciples was, "Where is your faith?"

Luke 8: 26-39 is the lesson in which Jesus casts out Legions of demon spirits from the demon possessed man. This healed man was told, "Go home and tell how much God has done for you."

Luke 8: 40-56 depicts two miracle lessons in one. First, the woman with the issue of blood for twelve years, who touched the hem of His garment and was healed, followed by the raising of Jairus' daughter from the dead. For this last one, He put everyone out of the room except His inner circle, Peter, James and John. He was trying to get them to a deeper understanding of who He was and to strengthen them, because He would no longer be with them in flesh form anymore.

Continuing the history of what happened before the well known feeding of the five thousand, after performing the miracles we just recounted, Jesus then took time to give the disciples instructions on how they were to go out and spread the message of salvation. And what they taught was to be accompanied by signs and wonders.

Now, the question that arises from this series of events is, after witnessing the many miracles, listening to and walking with Jesus, did the disciples understand who Jesus was? And the second question to ponder is, did they understand what they were called to be and to do as His disciples? I believe the remainder of the sermon will show us that the answer is no to both questions.

The first point of this message is that there was a demonstrated history of miracles that Jesus performed that should have lead the disciples to an understanding of who He was and an understanding of what He was empowering them to do. There should likewise be a history that promotes our growth and propels us to go forth with signs and wonders to win others to Christ.

2nd point: Jesus told the disciples, in verse Luke 9:13, "You feed them."

We now look at our focus scripture lesson, when Jesus fed the five thousand with two fish and five loaves of bread, with eyes open a little wider. We should understand that what Jesus said to the disciples in this lesson was intended to move them to action. He expected that they had learned something from all of the miracles He had already performed in their presence. So let's look at the challenge that was before them. Five thousand hungry men plus women and children are waiting and what do the disciples do? They present a suggestion to Jesus, in verse 12 that they disperse the gathering so that they could go and seek shelter and food for themselves. And again, we re-phrase the question, Did they understand who Jesus was? Do you and I live day by day with an understanding of who He truly is? I am suggesting that we don't? We have heard the account of this miracle for most of our lives and we have both read it and sang about it, but most of all, we have gained such strength in times of need from this miracle. We have strengthened our resolve to trust and depend on Him as our source, even during times when our cupboards are nearly bare. We lean on Him by faith during times when our worries and heartaches are mounting and we realize that our own strength is failing. What a lesson on how Jesus will always provide and how He can take what we have and make what He wants!

In verse 13 the disciples suggested that maybe they should go and buy meat for the people, because they only had the 5 loaves and two fish. These close followers of Christ were dumbfounded. So what did Jesus do? He gave them the menial task to have the people seated in groups of 50 and distribute the bread and fish (which He prayed to the Father and multiplied); and then He had them to take up the 12 baskets of left overs that remained after the meal. Does the Lord ever have to slow walk us into realizing the power He has instilled in us sometimes, because we just fail to step out on faith and do the things He has called us to do?

Let's revisit points 1 and 2 because point 3 takes a marked turn.

1. There is a history of miracles found in the Word of God that tells us who Jesus is and who we are to be in Him. There is also a history in your life and mine, which displays the power of God and we should be empowered by it to step out on faith.

2. While this miracle of the massive feeding is valuable for showing how Jesus can multiply what He has to work with in order to provide our every need, and He promised to do so, we also glean the fact that He is calling for us to do things ourselves and for others, by faith in Him. He said, "feed my people."

With these two points in mind, let's talk about "New Hands" and "New Feet", because what the disciples in the Bible didn't get, but we, today's disciples will get is that, "These feet were made for holiness". I have suggested that because the disciples failed to understand who Jesus was, they were unable to imagine how they could accomplish His work in the world. They were depending on Him to show up and do the work, and they were to be the crew that walked around with Him. **And they saw Him face-to-face.** So fast forward to today. We walk around this world proclaiming what Jesus did and still does, while we are not doing the things that He has shown us in His Word to do, just like the Bible's disciples. We walk as Bible toting, scripture quoting, Bible story reciting modern day disciples of God, with no power. We study all of the Greek and Roman history and the Greek and Hebrew words and even the political climate of the Bible days, but we don't fully grasp who He really is. And we are therefore unable to perform what He assigns for us to do. We are still waiting for Him to show up and get the work done, while we are the crew waiting around to say, "I told you who He was and what He would do." It brings to mind the first part of ***2 Timothy 3:5*** which says ***Having a form of godliness, but denying the power thereof:*** We realize that this verse is not referring to our having this godly outward appearance while failing to walk in the power and authority that comes with salvation, but the wording of the passage does lead us to think, should we be proclaiming His power without walking in His power as He says we should? Are you getting the third point yet? I am referencing "New Hands and New Feet" because your feet and mine were made for holiness. Your hands and mine were made for holiness.

Dig a little further to get this point. After Jesus fed the 5000, the Bible gives the account of Him praying privately and His disciples are still with Him. So He asks them "Who do men say that I am?" and

He got the various responses. Then He asks them, "Who do you say that I am?" This is when Peter makes his revelation statement, "Thou art the Christ, the Son of the Living God." Shortly after this, when Jesus is trying to prepare them for the fact that He must die to save mankind, Peter jumps in to protest against Jesus' death - showing that while he had a momentary flash of revelation, he still didn't understand what it means that Jesus is the Christ. He did not have the full, heart deep, soul penetrating, life changing understanding of what it all meant. And we still have limited understanding of it even now.

Believers, point #3 is when we accept Jesus as our Lord and Savior, as we grow in the spiritual knowledge, the revelation knowledge of who He is, we finally understand what "New Hands" and "New Feet" mean. Our new existence is tied up in the Trinity. Let's look at it. God, the

Father describes Him as creator. God, the Son describes the same creator having come into the world in flesh form (Jesus). God, the Holy Ghost describes the Creator and the Son having come in Spirit form and filling us, the believers. Believers, when we are saved, disciples of Christ, we are no longer to wait for Jesus to show up and do what needs to be done down here for us, because He is already here (living within us). We are to trust Him, pray to the Father, through Jesus, and He gives us "New hands and New Feet" to step out on faith and do the work that needs to be done. The Bible disciples could have performed the miracle themselves if they believed, understood, prayed, and stepped out on faith.

Now take a good look at your hands. Your hands are new! Take a good look at your feet. Your feet are new too! Allow me to get a little personal with this. I have shared with a few people how it was that I first discovered that God would use my hands for His glory. I had a son who was sick at birth, an extremely premature child, 2 lbs 14 ½ oz. I laid hands on my precious son and he was healed. He should be 30 years old when this is read. As I continue to grow in grace, God has made me profoundly aware of the power to bless people by a touch. I don't announce it every time, but I bless others often. Again I say, look at your hands and feet, people of God, because they really are new. **Luke 10:8-9** tells us that Jesus sent His disciples out and advised them to heal the sick where I send you and say unto them, "**the kingdom of God is come nigh unto you.**" New Hands.

Now take a good look at your feet. Your feet are new! Our feet were made for holiness. **Luke 10:10-11** Jesus told the disciples that as they went from place to place, if anyone did not receive them, wipe their dust off of them, because they actually didn't receive the kingdom of God, which had come nigh to them. See, because God's Spirit is now in you as a believer, wherever your feet trod, you are presenting the presence of God. Your feet are holy. "New Feet. It is my prayer that in looking more closely at some of these spiritual attributes of newness in Christ, we have been drawn just a little bit closer to Jesus. I also pray that the people of God will walk through our homes, schools, places of work, and within our churches knowing who we are and stepping out on faith to do what we have been called to do. And I declare that we will wait for His Spirit to unction us and then move, instead of waiting for Jesus to come back to this earth to do the work Himself.

We will always face decisions that must be made and challenges that must be dealt with. We will deal with family members and confusion, sickness and bills, gossip and anger. The fiery darts of the adversary are trained on us, but we are greater than our problems, because of who we are and whose we are and we need to tap into that greatness. Jesus will never stop sending His Word to teach us and mature us in this walk, so we will be s-t-r-e-t-c-h-e-d. I admit that I sometimes quiver to see that when the Word goes forth from God, then comes the stretching to seal it and work it within us. But I trust that you will find encouragement and strength from what Jesus told the disciples in verse 13 ***of Luke 9, "You go feed them yourselves."*** Remember, in ***Luke 9:55,*** after the people did not receive Jesus, the disciples wanted to know, "should we make fire come down from heaven and consume the people?" We are not to be that way, when we have His Spirit. He told them, ***"Ye know not what manner of Spirit ye are of."*** This sermon was sent so that we may know what manner of Spirit we are of. We are sent forth with New Hands and New Feet to do the work of the Father, not to consume those who have not yet come to the understanding that the kingdom of God has come nigh to them.

Let us go forward knowing that with New Hands we can touch that wayward child, that wavering spouse, or even that unpleasant co-worker. And no grand announcement is required, just the anointing of the Holy Ghost. Go forward knowing that with New Feet we can walk through our homes, facing confusion, fears, struggles, trials and bills, because everywhere our feet trod will be blessed and will know that the Holy Ghost has passed through to make the difference.

In closing, Jesus says to us today, "you do it". That declaration within itself means, The power I have, I have also given to you. Walk in it. If there is any doubt that this Word is true, refer to ***Luke***

10:19-20 which says, ***Behold, I give you power to tread on serpents and scorpions, and over all the power of the enemy: and nothing shall by any means hurt you. Notwithstanding in this rejoice not, that the spirits are subject unto you; but rather rejoice, because your names are written in heaven.***

Walking in the path set by Jesus only applies to those who are saved. It can only be done by the power of His Spirit. So if you have not accepted Jesus as Lord of your life, please know that now is the day of salvation. Jesus died on Calvary's cross to pay our sin debt. He loved us so much that, while we were yet sinners, He died for us. God, the Father, rose Jesus from the dead. He was witnessed by many before He ascended to the Father. Today, if you believe in Jesus, and confess with your mouth that God raised Him from the dead, you are saved. Pray and ask Him to forgive you of all of your sins.

It doesn't take a lot of fancy words, just sincere heart repenting. Pray for God to lead you to a good church, where His Word is both taught and lived. Invite Jesus to lead you all the way from earth to glory and He will, because you are now a part of our family. God bless you.

\\\\\\\\\\\\\\\\\\\\\\\\\\\\\\\\\\\\\\

FOR DISCUSSION

Chapter4

1. Did you find strength in reflecting on the miracles Jesus performed when He walked among man?
2. Do you believe that He has called us to do the things that He did when He was here? How do you know?
3. Did you remember that the invitation to salvation should always be extended, if we are on a mission for The Lord? Were you waiting for it?
4. Has the Lord worked miracles through you? Do you believe that He can work through you if you pray and surrender yourself to Him?
5. This chapter started with a discussion between God and the writer. Are you familiar with hearing the voice of the Lord? Are you searching the scriptures for directions in this area?
6. Research "the gifts of the Spirit" and

"the fruit of the Spirit" and discuss what each mean, in preparation for greater works.

7. Discuss Luke 9:17 of the sermon text and how God's provision was not just enough, but more than enough.

At the table of The Lord, we are filled to over-flowing! Give Him thanks and praise!

The Disgruntled Employee
Chapter 5

How many times in life have you found yourself upset or dissatisfied with the assignment that was given to you? I know that over the years I have been less than happy with many assignments I have received over the years.

Recently, I realized that God was bringing a lesson full circle for me. I was drawn into several conversations with people who were struggling with options of quitting or hanging in there during difficult times in ministry. It was particularly interesting, as I thought on each incident, to find that three very different people had three very different angles when they presented their dilemmas to me. Each were leaders in ministry and all were relatively new to leadership roles within their ministry.

The first leader presented her case

and she was struggling with trying to get programs off the ground. She had begun many programs for the youth department she was called to lead in her church and more often than not the programs would be canceled during planning. This young woman took full blame for each cancellation, even though she was not planning the programs alone. She was also not the person canceling them. She declared that she would press on with her work and remain positive, because she knew that God called her to this leadership role and she was depending on Him to lead her.

The second leader presented her case as she was struggling with a co-worker within her group who seemed to fight her on every decision she made. The second leader also declared that God called her and placed her in her position and with or without her co-worker she was pressing on. However, she also stated that the co-worker could just quit the organization if she was dissatisfied, as she was tired hearing her complain all the time and making trouble within the group.

The third leader presented her situation to me. This person had the complaint that she was being left out on decisions being made for her organization. She argued that holiness and spiritual growth was not a part of the decisions being made and within the programs being planned by the ministry where she served. She had attempted on several occasions to interject into the group the need for them to take seriously the assignment to edify the body so that they in turn would be able to spread the love of Jesus through their ministry, but all of her suggestions were rejected and she was now being left out of all plans completely. After much discussion, this leader stated that the other members could just have the organization and she would simply leave them alone. After extensive conversation, she knew that quitting was not the answer, because she also recognized that God called her to her ministry as well.

It is with mixed emotions that I must now admit that we could place my name under either of the three situations above as I have been all three. I have tried to plan things, had them canceled and wanted to give up at times and press on at other times. I have tried to lead, have members challenge me to no end and wanted to just ignore them and do my own thing or to retaliate against them and move on in some way. I have tried countless times to interject Jesus and His ways, His commands, His Spirit into planning programs that were supposed to be for His glory and have had everything I said rejected. I have felt defeated, wanted to throw in the towel and retreat to my own corner and let them have the whole thing. Since I am still here and am stronger and more determined than I have ever been, I guess I was a good person for these leaders to speak with. I could really relate to them. Add to that the fact that I really love all three or them and have known them for years. I could talk to them.

I won't go into further details concerning my friends, but I will say that they are doing just fine and are continuing to do a mighty work for the Lord. They are still learning and growing just as I am. Not one of them was defeated. In a word, they were referred to The Word, where they found the strength they needed and the direction for their ministries. I think it helped that when they came to me they didn't find someone who thought that she had arrived, but someone who is still arriving, still growing and being perfected day by day. Every day with Jesus is sweeter than the day before!

Let's take a look at a few passages of scripture that may help us all on this journey, as we commit ourselves to walking in the calling God has made on our lives.

Matthew 6:30-33 says, *Wherefore, if God so clothe the grass of the field, which to day is and to morrow is cast into the oven, shall he not much more clothe you, O ye of little faith? Therefore take no thought, saying, What shall we eat? Or, What shall we drink? Or, Wherewithal shall we be clothed? (For after all these things do the Gentiles seek:) for your heavenly Father knoweth that ye have need of these things. But seek ye first the kingdom of God, and his righteousness; and all these things shall be added unto you.*

This portion of scripture is so overused that it is often not carrying the full weight of it's meaning. We find listed here the things that we need as human beings for survival. It doesn't list the things that we could make it without, the amenities of life that we overlook. When we focus on what is said here and apply it to our calling, we could ask the question, Do we really think that God would give us an assignment and withhold the tools we need to accomplish His will for us? It would be helpful if we approach these dilemmas from the place called faith in God.

Jeremiah 29:11-12 says, ***For I know the thoughts that I think toward you, saith the Lord, thoughts of peace, and not of evil, to give you an expected end. Then shall ye call upon me, and ye shall go and pray unto me, and I will hearken unto you.***

Isn't it refreshing to reflect on the fact that God not only called you to be who you are striving to be, but that He actually has made plans for your success? There is no challenge that you are facing today that He is not only aware of but He has planned the outcome of it. The challenges do not change His plan, but they move His plans along.

When we find that our best made plans are canceled over and over again, sometimes due to poor planning or mistakes on our part and sometimes because of the actions of others, we must evaluate and re-evaluate how we came to the point where we are. But we must also recall that He is right there with us. Is it possible that He is trying to tell us something or better yet, to teach us something? What are we learning each time as we begin again? If we received the specific assignment from the Lord, then we must expect that He is there with us. It is counter-productive to keep questioning our call each time we are faced with challenges. We must be assured in our Spirit of our calling and never look back from it. We must also, however, evaluate where our ideas are originating from for the programs, out-reaches and other things we are planning. Remember the previous chapter in which we established the fact that God never commanded us to create any thing. That means that the plans have already been created. We must go to Him for the assignment and then stay before Him as we are planning and working His plan. Remember, we are the vessels. He is the Creator. Be patient with yourself as mistakes will be made, but don't give up on yourself, because God will never give up on you. Get in the Word and stay in the Word and press on toward the mark.

Now there will be times when we find that members we are working with are difficult to communicate with. Sometimes we don't understand them and they don't understand us either. We must remember as leaders that the group we are leading was not founded on us, nor for our glory. This is a very sensitive area, because we put so much of ourselves and our hearts into what we set out to do. I don't really think you would have been chosen if you were not one to put your full effort into what you do. This is not a bad thing. It is simply an area that has to remain before us so that we do not lose sight of God's leadership over ours. He doesn't leave us here to do things by ourselves, so we have to remain open to hear Him speaking to us through others he placed on the team with us to get the job done. Don't forget that working together is a part of His design for His people.

Consider ***Ephesians 4: 1-6 I therefore, the prisoner of the Lord, beseech you that ye walk worthy of the vocation wherewith ye are called, With all lowliness and meekness, with long-suffering, forbearing one another in love; Endeavoring to keep the unity of the Spirit in the bond of peace. There is one body, and one Spirit, even as ye are called in one hope of your calling; One Lord, one faith, one baptism, One God*** *and Father of all, who is above all, and through all, and in you all.*

And *Psalm 133* which says, *Behold how good and how pleasant it is for brethren to dwell together in unity!*

These awesome scriptures serve to remind us how God intends for us to work together and what attitude should be shown as we work for Him. This is a great way to bring glory to His name. And He is so worthy! Our Lord receives honor and glory and praise when we lead His people by His Spirit that it is worth it for each of us to go back to His word for direction and open our hearts to others.

There undoubtedly are times when we, as leaders, try to keep the focus of the group on the Lord. It is often our intent to use the organization we are serving to grow the body. We are eager to lead others who are already saved into a deeper relationship with our God. Aren't we striving for closer communion with Him ourselves? It is a great thing to see others grow as we grow. This is not something that can be forced on others and sometimes it is rejected. Please don't get discouraged. You are not alone. You just need to seek God's voice to know how to gently lead others in this way. Often times a sermon is much better when seen in our lives instead of preached vocally. Don't worry, it wasn't too long ago when none of us were very deep and I still don't think I'm deep now. I am willing to learn more and grow more each day though, and I pray that my lack of depth isn't causing someone else a real problem. Remember we are all in this together. Don't give up. The Word says, that He will take us from glory to glory. He will do it, in His time and in His way. When faced with rejection while trying your best to do your best, take a look at the familiar passage..

Isaiah 54:17 No weapon that is formed

against thee shall prosper; and every tongue that shall rise against thee in judgment thou shalt condemn. This is the heritage of the servants of the Lord, and their righteousness is of me, saith the Lord. How about that!

We often quote the first part, but look again at the second part. Your righteousness is of the Lord. That means that you are not sent to prove anything to anyone. The Word teaches that He is not a respecter of persons. The same thing He is doing in your life, you can rest assured He will do in the lives around you. He feels your concern and He indeed is the answer. Continue working for the Lord and let His light shine through you. When light enters a room, it casts out darkness...

I started this writing by stating that recently a lesson given to me was brought full circle and that was what inspired me to begin to write. Several years ago, I was given an assignment and it meant that I was to meet with and speak with every organization in my church. I was to speak with each leader and then with each group. Wow! The Lord gave me much Word to deliver and quite the audience, or so I thought. The assignment was just to share tools for the groups to work together in unity to plan their programs and to encourage them to reach out to other members of the church to work with them. I tried to accomplish the task at hand for some time, but I found that people were not excited about what I had to say. And they certainly were not welcoming or willing to change their ways of doing things. Needless to say, I became discouraged and I stopped trying for a time. Oh, I never stopped working hard in the church, but I was no longer trying to get others to work together, at least not in an organized way. I adopted the attitude of the third leader I introduced and thought "they could just have their organizations." When the three leaders presented their cases to me and I again was faced with addressing the same issues I was trying to address when the assignment was originally given to me, I could only shake my head as I had a little talk with Jesus. I would like to think that He realized that when I was faced with the challenges and the rejection that came with the assignment, I acted just like a disgruntled employee. I have planned to meet with a couple of organizations now and I still have all of the paperwork God gave me when I first took the assignment. I received a new charge of determination to make the difference that is needed, because I can see so clearly that this is needed. Everyone can't do this kind of work. It has to be someone who has "been there - done that" and is still learning and growing and not ashamed to admit it. Thank God that He doesn't give up on us when we become disgruntled employees.

Don't be surprised to find that the ministry you were called to work is not a one man show. It is usually not the way God intended, because He tells us to work in unity over and over throughout His word.

So as we move forward in obedience to the calling on our lives, a selection from scripture I have found most helpful is found in,

1 Corinthians 12:14-20 For the body is not one member, but many. If the foot shall say, Because I am not the hand, I am not of the body; is it therefore not of the body? And if the ear shall say, Because I am not the eye, I am not of the body; is it therefore not of the body? If the whole body were an eye, where were the hearing? If the whole were hearing, where were the smelling? But now hath God set the members every one of them in the body, as

it hath pleased him. And if they were all one member, where were the body? But now are they many members, yet but one body.

FOR DISCUSSION

Chapter 5

1. Have you ever found yourself in the position of a disgruntled employee? If so, what gave you the strength to press on through that difficult time?

2. Locate at least three passages of scripture that you may reference for encouragement during times when someone may think of throwing in the towel, and discuss them.

3. Set aside a week to commit the three scriptures from question #2 to memory.

4. Do others feel that you are someone to whom they can come and share their concerns with? If so, have you provided words of encouragement or have you joined in the complaints or concerns? Take time to examine how God can use you in this area.

5. Do you most often complete your assignments or is there a pattern of giving up when challenges and frustration comes?

6. How has your choices helped or hurt others around you?

7. In retrospect, would you make the same choices today that you may have made several years ago? Refer to questions 4, 5, and 6 and apply this question to each.

8. Are you able to place a period after your past choices and move forward, with a little more wisdom?

9. Were there times when God used repeated frustration, failure, and obstacles as tools for telling you to stop and change directions on an assignment?

10. Did you remember that the Word did not come to condemn you, but to give you

life, as you reflected on past decisions from the questions above?

What is God Asking of Me? What Am I Asking of God?

CHAPTER 6

> *12 "I beseech you therefore, brethren, by the mercies of God, that ye present your bodies a living sacrifice, holy, acceptable unto God, which is your reasonable service.*
> *2 And be not conformed to this world: but be ye transformed by the renewing of your mind, that ye may prove what is that good, and acceptable, and perfect, will of God.*
> *3 For I say, through the grace given unto me, to every man that is among you, not to think of himself more highly than he ought to think; but to think soberly, according as God hath dealt to every man the measure of faith..."*

Whenever I would hear a sermon based on a single word of a scripture, I would internally shut down. This was for two reasons. First, based on my own practice of Bible study, in that I never studied a specific word out of the scripture and professed to have received the intent of God from that one word. Second, I must admit that I have heard so many take one word and go from there, without scripture that support the points of the message. I am so thankful that the God we serve doesn't leave us in that condition, when we do that. God is one who continues to work with us even when we shut down, like I used to do. It's a blessing to know that He is ever changing us and the way that we think. When He first built this sermon from one word "be", I knew that in His own way He was laughing at me. He was continuing to do a work in me. But on a serious level, this time I realized that God doesn't think it is cute when we continue to show that we can't get it, meaning get His lessons, until He has to make it personal for us like this. Instead, He has told us that we are to have the willing attitude to receive the Word and search the scriptures daily, just as the people of Berea in the book of Romans. Isn't it a wonderful thing to have a loving Father, though, who has His own way of continually addressing those areas within us that need to change? He molds us, re-shapes us, sometimes shaves off the jagged edges and smooths us out, as He transforms His own. And He does it through His Word. He says, ***be ye transformed by the renewing of your mind.***

Today, we find that there is much to be said concerning that one word, "be", because that word is powerful enough to change the whole meaning of the scripture, as small as it is. We must spend a little time with the supporting verses, because they are what makes "be" so important. The 1st verse is the preamble to the command to come. So let us study the Word.

Vs 1 says, ***I beseech you therefore, brethren, by the mercies of God, that ye present your bodies a living sacrifice, holy, acceptable unto God, which is your reasonable service.***

Points from this scripture:

1. This statement and intended action is directed to believers. We know this because it is impossible for an unbeliever to present his body as a living sacrifice. Consider what we already know from scripture. The requirement for a sacrifice is that it must be perfect, without blemish. Therefore, an unforgiven, unrepentant sinner cannot present himself as a perfect sacrifice.

2. Presenting ourselves means willingly offering ourselves for transformation by our Lord. Accepting the truth of our imperfection in the flesh, covered by the perfection of Christ is what makes us holy and acceptable to God, and the verse goes on to explain that this is our reasonable

service.

Let's dig a little deeper into the two statements of fact. Let's begin with the un-forgiven sinner, mentioned in the first point. In the Old Testament, the perfect living sacrifice was killed and then the blood of the sacrifice was used ceremonially for payment of the sin debt of the people, by presentation before God. For this same reason, there was no one worthy to pay our sin debt in full, except Jesus, the perfect one, the only one who was without sin. At Calvary, Jesus was the perfect sacrifice who was also killed to pay our sin debt. These facts lend us the understanding that only someone who is saved could present himself a living sacrifice, and that is only because we are covered by the blood of Jesus.

Both humility and reality may cause those who are saved to question how they are to present their bodies a living sacrifice. When we believe, confess, and accept Jesus (the perfect, pure, holy sacrifice) as our Lord and we become saved, we are covered by the blood (that He shed to pay our sin debt). This is what makes the believer eligible to present his body a living sacrifice. God does not see us as we are (imperfect); He sees us through the blood of Jesus.

In the second point, we admit that we are not perfect people. We are **perfected** (covered) people. It is a myth to think that when one is saved, he becomes perfect in his flesh.

2 Corinthians 5:17-19 Therefore if any may be in Christ, he is a new creature: old things are passed away; behold, all things are become new. And all things are of God, who hath reconciled us to himself by Jesus Christ, and hath given to us the ministry of reconciliation. The passing away of old things here is referring to the old sin, the old man which passes away in the forgiveness of Jesus afforded by the blood payment He made for us. All things are become new, a new beginning, new life. These instructions in Romans, which continue the salvation plan of transformation, give us the road-map to allow God to continue the work that began at salvation. If 2 Corinthians meant that we no longer act on our flesh or commit sin in deed and thought, then the transformation we are commanded to allow in Romans would not be needed.

We do not immediately begin to think like Jesus and speak like He did and behave in ways that line up with our new life, by some supernatural act that occurs in a moment of time, when we become saved. We do not immediately begin to have miracles worked through us or to fully understand the spiritual interpretation of scripture, referred to as ***rightly dividing the Word of truth,*** in 2 Timothy 2:15. Not at all. Most will admit that we are not perfect people. We are a work in progress, even after we are saved. The work in progress part is what Romans is giving us instructions for. The Word goes on to say ***holy, acceptable unto God, which is your reasonable service***, in that first verse.

In summary of verse 1, When we believe, confess, and accept Jesus (the perfect, pure, holy sacrifice) as our Lord and we become saved, we are covered by the blood (that He shed to pay our sin debt). This is what makes the believer eligible to present his body a living sacrifice.

See ***Jude vs. 24 Now unto him that is able to keep you from falling, and to present you faultless before the presence of his glory with exceeding joy...***

God does not see us as we are (imperfect); He sees us through the blood of Jesus. Again, we are not perfect people. We are **perfected** (covered) people.

Now our transformation begins with verse 2 and it is a two part work, with an end of glorifying God. Let's see what it says. After the believer willingly presents himself for the work to be done within him, this verse says, ***And be not conformed to this world:*** Here we find this little two letter word, "be". The meaning of this word within the context of this one verse of scripture is that this is a word of surrender, not a word of action on our part. We surrender willingly for the new Spirit within us as believers to Stop The Process of Conforming to the Things of This World. The Word says, Be Not. Verse 2 tells us what the Spirit does within us. Let's take this into real life and see it at work, now. From the time we are born into this world of sin, everything around us has been working a process of conforming us to the world's ways of thinking, believing and behaving and the world's views of right and wrong, good and evil. We see all of the advertisements that tell us what we want, even when those things are not necessarily what God wants for us. We are taught to compete against each other and strive to be the best when the Word tells us to work together. He will exalt us in due time. We learn in this world to go after what we want, even if someone else is more deserving. We learn how to perfect the art of "not saying what we really mean", the skills of manipulation (as long as we can never be pinned down). Oh, this list is by far too big to attempt to cover the many forms of sin we have been a part of in the world prior to salvation. We each would have to take a look at ourselves and assess things in our own world to deal with sin. The point from the Word is that when we surrender to the new Spirit we received at salvation, we give The Holy Ghost free reign to stop this process within us of conforming to sin. What we must learn from this one word "be" is that many of us as believers make so many unnecessary mistakes because we are trying to do something ourselves, due to an understanding of this scripture based on face value and not Spirit revelation. We often begin to act out against the world's views before we are equipped to do so, because we are doing a work in ourselves, when the work He told us to do was in verse 1, present ourselves, willingly surrender ourselves. Oh, we get excited and go into our homes and address our poor spouses and children, "in the name of Jesus" we say, when part 2 of the verse hasn't even started. This can begin conflicts in the home that God never intended to be there. We often begin to offend those who should be growing and changing with us, because the work in us is only beginning. A good way of understanding this is to remember when you were a very young child and the parent said, come to the tub because your hair needs to be washed. Who washed your hair? She said "come and be washed" you came and she washed. Well look at it that way. The Lord is saying, "come (present yourself) and be washed (He washes us). How about, your hair needs to Be not styled, but Be washed. Be not styled required no action on your part, just like Be Not Conformed.

Part 2 says, ***but be ye transformed by the renewing of your mind,.*** This little word "be" shows up again and it means the same thing. The Spirit of God does the transforming work stated in this verse. At least in this section, it is easy for us to see that we are unable to go into our own inside and change things like transformers. Otherwise, I truly believe that we would be performing physical surgery on ourselves trying to change. The result would be even more disastrous than the actual attempts not to conform to this world. At least with that part, we aren't killing families, friends, neighbors and others physically by offending them. We are sometimes breaking up otherwise good relationships with our good intentions. The Spirit does this transforming work though, and thank God for sparing our lives with this. That segment does indeed interject a portion for us to do. It says that He (the Holy Ghost) renews our minds. This is where we work with the New Spirit within us. We are to read the Word of God. We are to fill those places left open as the Spirit stops that conforming process of worldly things implanting themselves with us when we surrender, with the Good News now available to us as believers. The Word supports this in the full text of ***2 Timothy 2:15 Study to shew thyself approved unto God, a workman that needeth not to be ashamed, rightly dividing the word of truth.*** And there are countless scriptures that tell us to get in this Word and study.

The end of this verse says, ***that ye may prove what is that good, and acceptable,***

and perfect, will of God. This is simply stating that with this transformation process, our lives will show forth openly what God's will displays in the life of a true believer. When we allow Him to change us, to transform us through His Spirit, we will begin to walk like He intended, talk like He intended, do the things that He commanded us to do for His glory. We will be the proof of the truth of His Word, as we live down here in this world ... in the world, but not of the world.

Finally, my brothers and sisters, in the Lord's service, this final verse concludes that we are not to think of ourselves more highly than we ought to think. When we become so high minded in our thoughts concerning ourselves, it is more difficult for us to accept that we are still imperfect people who need to have that covering of the blood of Jesus. When we are existing in this unreasonable state of living with ourselves, knowing full well that we are still committing sin, and yet unable to admit that, even to ourselves, we become unable to present our bodies a living sacrifice for God to continually work the work of transformation within us. The reasonable service mentioned in verse one, refers to coming before Him with the truth of who we are, and the truth that even now, we still need Jesus.

See the last part of the verse tells us where the measure of faith we have came from, not from ourselves, but from God. Therefore no man can boast. We must remain humble. Then and only then can we accept the blood covering, present ourselves and "be" ye transformed.

In answer to the questions What is God asking of me? Surrender and stop fighting to change yourself. **What am I asking of God?** Transform my life, my Lord! Show me how to trust You to do the Work first in me and then through me.

At the beginning of this sermon, we

established that this Word was speaking to the believer. So it is now that I ask the question, do you want your life to be changed today forever? Well this Word declared that Jesus died on Calvary's cross for the sins of man. He paid your sin debt in full. And God raised Him from the dead, after the debt was paid. If you believe this, and confess it with your mouth, then ask Jesus to forgive you of your sins, based on what He did for you. Accept Jesus as Lord of your life today. Then this Word, explaining the process of transformation for the rest of your life is yours.

Bless The Lord!

//////////////////////////////////

Let us apply this Word to the call on our lives today. Any assignment that God has given us will become easier to complete and will yield greater fruit, as we surrender more fully to Him and allow Him to transform us. Every challenge that we face will be met with more knowledge, wisdom, and understanding as we continue to grow with God. Isn't it good to know that He will continue the work He started in us?

Early this morning when I rose to get ready for another day at work, the television was on and I was blessed to wake up to a world wide preacher beginning to deliver words of encouragement for the new day. By the way, this was the morning after I wrote the sermon you just read. Behold, this woman of God was explaining how our Lord changes us day by day, as we surrender to His will and His way of living. I was immediately drawn into what she was delivering, as I sat there with my mouth wide open. She was not coming from Romans 12, but the message was the same. The main point of her message was "oh, what peace we often forfeit, all because we do not carry everything to God in prayer". She expounded on the fact that when God is working a new work within us, we are able to tell that we are changing, when we reach that place of peace with the change He has made. For example, if you are one who gossips and this sinful behavior is removed, as God reveals to you that it does not line up with who He called you to be, when you finally have received that newness of life it doesn't cause you to lose your peace when you hear someone else gossip. During the process of transforming, you may begin to constantly address the behavior of others who you hear gossiping, but it usually will come across to them as judgmental and your interference may be rejected. But when you come to the place where you are free from that sin in your life and you are no longer struggling against it, you will be better able to gently lead others away from it in more subtle ways, such as not joining in or changing the subject, as opposed to directly addressing the sin. What we learn as God is molding and re-shaping our lives is how He does it gently and patiently. Many times He has made changes in us and we can't even recall when we stopped doing some things that were simply a part of who we were.

FOR DISCUSSION

Chapter 6

1. Did you receive the significance of the word "be" within the scripture lesson?

2. Have you identified things that lead you to mentally shut down, whenever you hear them or see them?

3. Discuss the authority that you have to take command of your response to those things that shut you down? Search the scriptures and find those verses that tell about your authority in the world. Remember that authority over your own life choices is included.

4. Have you surrendered and presented yourself to God, willingly, for transformation or are there areas where you find you are still fighting Him for control?

5. What does it mean to be covered by the

blood of Jesus?

6. Have you fully accepted the forgiveness of God for your past sins or are you still holding yourself guilty? If you are still carrying guilt in your heart today, stop where you are and confess that to God in prayer, and ask Him to renew your mind so that you may accept His forgiveness.

7. Are you certain of confirmation from God that you are rightly dividing The Word? Discuss the ways God uses to confirm His truth for you. Do you sometimes use The Word to affirm your personal opinions?

8. Discuss how being perfected is immediate, while changing through transformation is a progressive work? Explain how transformation works.

____

____

Never Be Afraid to Seek More and More

Chapter 7

1 Chronicles 4:9-10

9 And Jabez was more honourable than his brethren: and his mother called his name Jabez, saying, Because I bare him with sorrow.
10 And Jabez called on the God of Israel, saying, Oh that thou wouldest bless me indeed, and enlarge my coast, and that thine hand might be with me, and that thou wouldest keep me from evil, that it may not grieve me! And God granted him that which he requested..."

One thing that is needed for someone to be effective in whatever endeavor they set themselves to accomplish is continuous growth. It is quite amazing how much we can change and grow over time. We often experience growth spurts many times through life. It certainly is notable in children. It just looks like one day they have shot up substantially. All parents notice it when it is time for back-to-school shopping. How did the shoe size go up by a complete size over the short summer? And then, none of the pants from last school year come down lower than the child's ankle. They grew over the summer without our even noticing. And what about how they seem to suddenly grow in maturity. I don't think there is a parent alive who hasn't been surprised to find that a little one understood exactly what they meant when they thought they were speaking "over the child's head". Ha!

Well, the same thing happens in Christianity. There are certainly times when growth is so apparent that it seems to have happened over-night. We are going to look at a few scriptures that lead us to continuous steady growth. This is needed, because just as there are notable periods of growth, there are also times where time seems to stand still.

During these times, some begin to question why it seems they are not hearing from the Lord. One may wonder why they started out with such vigor and seem to have slowed to a trickle. Nobody running a long race does so at the same pace throughout the race. Every runner must pace himself. So during those times when we seem to be slowing down, and it's not a peaceful thing, it is helpful to know that we may encourage ourselves in the Word. This is needed, because we must never become complacent with no growth, no mission, and no vision.

We know that God knows how much each of us can handle, so we can rest assured that seeking growth will not lead us into trouble. Consider what happened when Moses requested to see the glory of God (***Exodus 33:18***). The Lord said to him in..

Exodus 33:20-23 And he said, Thou canst not see my face: for there shall no man see me, and live. And the Lord said, Behold, there is a place by me, and thou shalt stand upon a rock: And it shall come to pass, while my glory passeth by, that I will put thee in a clift of the rock, and will cover thee with my hand while I pass by: And I will take away mine hand, and thou shalt see my back parts: but my face shall not be seen.

God will give us what we need, but never too much for us to use for His glory. And that's a good place to start.

Jabez is not mentioned many times in the Bible, but I thought these two little verses would be a good point of focus, because so much is revealed in these few words. Right in the middle of listing all of the family members of Jabez, this 9th verse inserts a brief description of him, saying that he was more honourable than his brothers. The the 10th verse goes on to give us his prayer in which he asks the Lord to enlarge his coast. These verses summon us to first question motive in asking for more, seeking more growth.

Simply put, Jabez was honorable and we need to be honorable as people who are doing a work for the Lord. We need to seek higher learning, deeper understanding, more revelation, with the honorable intent of becoming of greater service to the Lord, through serving others.

It is said, "to whom much is given, much is required". It appears that Jabez knew that with much blessings came much responsibility, as in that 10 verse before asking God to enlarge his coast, he asked God to bless him indeed. He then asked for God's hand to be with him, which is really needed. When we receive the blessing, He extends our reach in service, we need Him to have His hand with us. It is not a wonder that the very next thing we see here is ***and that thou wouldest keep me from evil, that it may not grieve me!*** Oh this is also needed as the attacks will come, sometimes from within ourselves. Again, we are to be honorable in our requests. Are we seeking to satisfy self or to serve God and others. Jabez was honorable and ***God granted him that which he requested.***

Isn't it easy reading to go through the various Psalms, with their poetic flow? They may provide some of the most frequently quoted verses of scripture. Many of us learned the 23rd Psalm as one of the first things we memorized. Many parents begin by teaching it to their children at a young age. We all may run to the 27th Psalm in times of trouble and everyone knows, ***Let every thing that hath breath praise the Lord. Praise ye the Lord. Psalm 150:6.***

From here we readily run to the New Testament, where all of the miracles come to life, as visual reminders of the mighty hand of our Lord. But the entire Bible is so rich and there are so many passages we may only read, when we are determined to read the Bible from cover to cover. I can honestly say that I have heard countless sermons and there are many areas that I have never heard brought forth. It would benefit us all to re-evaluate how we look at the Word, because our God is not partial, but whole, and we are warned about taking it in part only.

See *Revelation 22: 18-19 For I testify unto every man that heareth the words of the prophesy of this book, If any man shall add unto these things, God shall add unto him the plagues that are written in this book: And if any man shall take away from the words of the book of this prophecy, God shall take away his part out of the book of life, and out of the holy city, and from the things which are written in*

this book. I may as well just admit to you that I love it! I love it because it attests to the fact the "Whole Word" is truth. So, I take this time to suggest to all that when we receive parts of the Word and we present only those parts, while not seeking to understand the whole, we are indeed taking away parts of the whole. So I encourage every believer not to become complacent with partial Word, while ignoring the whole. Some chapters and books may be easier reading than others and even more enjoyable, depending upon what we like as individuals, but we need to seek more than just what satisfies our flesh. We need to seek to be of greater service to God and others.

So I ask us each to ask ourselves, are we longing to satisfy our God and fulfill our calling? Or are we simply satisfied where we are? Do we understand that the more we seek Him, and He is His Word, the more we avail Him to use us for His glory. See

John 1:1 In the beginning was the Word, and the Word was with God, and the Word was God. The Word testifies of Him, Jesus. See ***John 5:39 Search the scriptures; for in them ye think ye have eternal life: and they are they which testify of me.*** We are told by Him to search Him (The Word). This is not just a command to simply read the Word, though. He went on to say in verse ***40 And ye will not come to me, that ye might have life.***

See, we have to know the Whole Word. Verse 39 is not just saying search the scriptures, but before that he says that they did not have the word ***abiding*** in them because they would not **receive Him**. So it is saying that by much reading and searching we still will not find the "more" we seek, if we still will not come to Him to receive life. Reading without yielding our understanding to Him, for revelation, will not produce life. We are not to seek more "word knowledge" for the purpose of knowledge. That is self-serving. But when we seek greater knowledge, wisdom and understanding ***through*** Him, for service to Him, He will grant the request to enlarge our coast. We must be like Jabez, more honorable.

Hosea 4:6-7 ***My people are destroyed for lack of knowledge: because thou has rejected knowledge, I will also reject thee, that thou shalt be no priest to me: seeing thou hast forgotten the law of thy God, I will also forget thy children.*** See our calling may begin on this path of perishing, if we reject knowledge of God. And the rejection may have a lasting effect. Do you remember that God told the Israelites to teach His Word to their children. And are you willing to search the scriptures for the passage that tells us that "then a generation rose up that did not know the Word" because of the lack of obedience by their parents to teach them? There are lasting effects of partial Word instead of whole Word. So let us each purpose, with honorable intent, to forget the past and press on toward the mark. I know you can find that one. Be encouraged as we seek more together, that we already know some things. Get excited about where you are now in Christ, from where you were ten years ago. Look at how He is using you today. And get even more excited about digging deeper in The Word, expecting to be of greater availability to God. Oh, the harvest is plenteous, but the laborers are few. Do not be afraid to seek more.

There are many scriptures to help us in our quest. See ***Philippians 2: 5-9*** How can we have the mind of God if we reject His Word? It isn't possible. We find in these verses that when Jesus humbled Himself and became obedient, God in turn exalted Him. He will also exalt you, when you seek Him humbly. ***2 Corinthians 11:3 But I fear, lest by any means, as the***

serpent beguiled Eve through his subtilty, so your minds should be corrupted from the simplicity that is in Christ.

Salvation and the things of God are not intended to trick us or confuse us. It is not some sign of great intellect either and should not be used for self elevation. So we must not be fooled by the tricks of the devil and shy away from the Word. The intent is always the mission we were all assigned to. Become fishers of men. But God does not want us satisfied with ignorance of His Word. We need to know Him better and we ought to want to know all that He wants to reveal to us. Let's equip ourselves to hear Him more clearly and to be able to rightly divide the Word of truth. I know you know where that scripture is located.

Ephesians 4:23 And be renewed in the spirit of your mind. How about that one. As we open ourselves for newness in the spirit of our mind, we free the Lord to use us in any way that He chooses. We ought to get excited about where He will lead us in another ten years.

As I focus on all of the verses in this chapter, my mind goes to the countless numbers that were added to the church in the book of Acts. What a work for the kingdom was done. Don't you want to be a part of those victories for Our Lord? And it can be done even now, if we are willing to let the Lord lead us into deeper things through His Word.

Finally, I end with these words of encouragement found in ***2 Peter 3:9 The Lord is not slack concerning his promise, as some men count slackness; but is long-suffering to us-ward, not willing that any should perish, but that all should come to repentance.*** I say to you, my brethren, let us go after the "all" referred to in this verse. God is long-suffering toward us. He knows that we should have been in His Word seeking a long time ago, but He really does want to use us all for the cause of Christ. So I am lead to suggest that if we each sincerely repent that we didn't dig into His Word and seek Him the way we should have long ago, He is faithful to forgive us and cleanse us and He will grant our request for more of Him.

> *"But without faith it is impossible to please him: for he that cometh to God must believe that he is, and that he is a rewarder of them that diligently seek him.." Hebrews 11:6*

Never be afraid to seek more and more. I am seeking right with you!

FOR DISCUSSION

Chapter 7

1. Are you seeking to be of greater service to God and others?

2. Are you seeking a closer walk with The Lord, or have you become complacent where you are?

3. Have you examined yourself and found that there are parts of the Bible where your attention is more focused, while there are others you are neglecting?

4. Are you able to do the assessment of where you are right now, for the purpose of motivating yourself to press harder to grow in Christ, without judging yourself harshly? Are you able to do the same for others?

5. Read ***Hosea 4:6.*** Discuss or meditate on how the lack of knowledge, results in the people perishing? Discuss how gaining knowledge may provide greater access to Godly wisdom.

6. Can we have the mind of God, while rejecting any portion of His Word? Why or Why not?

7. ***2 Peter 3:9*** says that The Lord desires that all would come to repentance. In your ministry, are you seeking all men, or a select group? Will you allow God to enlarge your reach today?

____

____

____

____

Taking It From Genesis to Revelation

Chapter 8

Some of the most wonderful characteristics of a Christian is that a Christian never stops learning, growing and improving. Oh, *everyone* grows. To live is to grow and to change, in human terms. But after your new birth, you really begin to live! That's what came to mind while I was receiving the Word for chapter 7. As God poured into my Spirit the revelation concerning how we need to digest the whole of His Word, He was truly dealing with me personally, so that is where we will begin **Taking it From Genesis to Revelations.**

God said to me, put your money where your mouth is. I was charged up by that Word and immediately began my self examination, which was what God was encouraging us all to do. I was lead to more closely look at the areas where my time and effort were deficient in my study of the Bible. So, before I could write another word, I found myself spending some time in those areas of the Old Testament that needed more of my attention. Let me readily confess that I am an avid reader, because I enjoy the art of reading, so over the years I have read the many details found in the Old Testament for the building of the ark, the temples and the altars.

So let me remind all who will read this that we are not looking for reading for the purpose of reading. We are looking to read the Word for the purposes of coming to know God better and for equipping ourselves for His mission. My first Pastor used to say, "You can't teach what you don't know and you can't lead where you don't go." Let's apply that wisdom and receive, "I will get closer to God through His Word and lead others to Him through His Word." I received that.

Since we are people of faith, we know that there is no reality in believing in chance happenings. Reality is that God is fully orchestrating our growth and decisions, as He preps us for greater service. This chapter will help to get us going where He is leading. We all know that the Bible has the two divisions of Old Testament and New Testament. It is further divided into ten sections:

Old Testament

New Testament

The Books of the Law-Pentateuch

History-Gospels

Genesis to Deuteronomy

Matthew to John

History

Church History

Joshua to Esther

Acts

Books of Poetry

Paul's Letters

Job to Song of Solomon

Romans to Philemon

Major Prophets

General Letters

Isaiah to Daniel

Hebrews to Jude

Minor Prophets

Revelation-Prophecies

Hosea to Malachi

Revelation

Looking at the Bible from this vantage point makes it easier for one to assess where he is now and where he will go from here. The task does not appear to be insurmountable, but interesting.

The enemy would have you to believe that the details found in the Old Testament are not of value as you go forth to win souls to Christ, because salvation is by grace through faith in Jesus ***(Ephesians 2:8)***, but he is wrong as usual. The Word of God is the Word of God and we find that He is both Alpha and Omega, Genesis through Revelation. The Word provides strength, knowledge, and revelation for the call on your life and mine.

Ecclesiastes 7:12 For wisdom is a defence, and money is a defence: but the excellency of knowledge is, that wisdom giveth life to them that have it.

Deuteronomy 30:19 I call heaven and earth to record this day against you, that I have set before you life and death, blessing and cursing: therefore choose life, that both thou and thy seed may live:

Let us look closely at the two scriptures listed, for in them the soul that seeks to hear from God may find direction. Ecclesiastes is comparing wisdom with money. We find that we may gain all of the money in this world, but money does not give life. Wisdom gives life. Most would agree that money without life is equal to an inheritance for one's children, in the natural. Money without life in the spirit is the equivalent of "gaining the whole world and losing one's soul". Deuteronomy reminds us that we have choices and that first choice doesn't say life or money as if they are opposites. Indeed, the opposite of life is death and the opposite of money is no money. This makes the choice of the two scriptures interesting. Ecclesiastes shows that both wisdom and money are assets as they are both described as defenses, but the scripture leads one to choose wisdom over money, because with wisdom comes life. Money can't buy you life. Then Deuteronomy supports, choose life. We return our thoughts to the characteristics of a Christian. We live, grow and improve.

We choose to gain wisdom and wisdom gives life, according to the scripture. The challenge we are dealing with is to study the whole of God's Word. One point we must accept is that wisdom is a gift of God and it is not the same thing as knowledge. All who have the ability to read with comprehension will gain knowledge. For this cause, there are many who know the Bible and can teach the Bible and even proclaim it's historical meaning. But the Word cautions us that when the anti-Christ comes many will be fooled, because he will be quite knowledgeable. Read the description of the great tribulation to come, found in *Matthew 24.*

Matthew 24:24 For there shall arise false Christs, and false prophets, and shall shew great signs and wonders; insomuch that, if it were possible, they shall deceive the very elect. For this reason, it is imperative that we understand that knowledge is not wisdom. Gaining knowledge does not give life. Wisdom, which comes from God, gives life. See *James 1:5 If any of you lack wisdom, let him ask of God, that giveth to all men liberally, and upbraideth not; and it shall be given him.* God is Spirit and by His Spirit, He gives life. So why are we encouraged to read and study more, if much reading and studying is equal to gaining knowledge? The clarification is that "revelation knowledge" is wisdom. We read to get to know Him better, as He reveals His Word to us. We must ask Him for wisdom to do the work of The Lord.

Proverbs 4: 5-7 Get wisdom, get understanding: forget it not; neither decline from the words of my mouth. Forsake her not, and she shall preserve thee: love her, and she shall keep thee. Wisdom is the principal thing; therefore get wisdom: and with all thy getting get understanding. This can only be achieved when we invoke the Spirit of God.

There is another old saying that I

remember from my youth. It is "Good things in, good things come out. Bad things in, bad things come out". As I became older and in salvation began to read the Word of God with the Spirit, I found that ***Luke 11:33-39*** addresses the lightness and darkness of the whole body. It explains that if the whole body is full of light then the whole shall be full of light, and will give thee light. But when thy eye is evil, thy body also is full of darkness. There are many other passages that reflect the same sentiment. So I use this example to transition our focus to another point we should gain in our search for a closer walk with God. There were many little sayings that I heard as a child and found scriptural basis for them as an adult. This fact made me realize and respect the wisdom of our parents, grand-parents and ancestors. It is noted that they had the wisdom to know how to take what they understood in their Spirit, from the

Word and present it in a manner that others could receive the message. Often times, as we learn more and more of the Bible, we lose the ability to relate to every day people who may not be Bible quoting people and what we offer is rejected. In other words, people shut down and can't receive what we are offering. This is just an example of gaining Bible knowledge, not Godly wisdom. So as we seek to full our inner selves with "good things", we must seek Godly wisdom, not just Bible knowledge. We seek wisdom, because wisdom gives life. We declare that we want to go forward, walking in the calling on our lives, bringing life to others. That's greater service to The Lord.

Let us take another look at Genesis to Revelation. Our God is both Alpha and Omega, the beginning and the end. The Word proclaims He is the I Am that I Am, which means God Is, meaning with no actual beginning and ending. He just is.

What we find when we stand back from the Word and receive Him in His intent is that Genesis points us to Revelation and Revelation points us to Genesis. In the beginning, God created all things perfectly and in the end all things will again be perfect. All scripture in between point to the same.

Revelation 21:1-3 And I saw a new heaven and a new earth: for the first heaven and the first earth were passed away; and there was no more sea. And I John saw the holy city, new Jerusalem, coming down from God out of heaven, prepared as a bride adorned for her husband. And I heard a great voice out of heaven saying, Behold, the tabernacle of God is with men, and he will dwell with them, and they shall be his people, and God himself shall be with them, and be their God. This takes us right back to the creation in Genesis. From the creation, it was all good. And from the fall of man unto the Revelation, we have been going back to Genesis. It is of great value to come to know God through all of the Word in between, as they are leading us back to the beginning and we need to lead others.

It is a great privilege to be chosen by God for service. Have you found out what He is calling you to do on this mission? Getting in the Word will help in learning to hear His voice and heed His call on your life. It gives us food to sustain us for the journey, because it is an awesome responsibility we have been afforded. Many will pass this way with much knowledge to share with others. As God gives light to us through His Word, we must stay with Him and in His Word for sustenance, to be effective fishers of men. Let us pray for oneness of mind and Spirit, as we make if from Genesis to Revelation.

Dear Father, we are thankful for the call on our lives to serve You. We humbly confess that we need You more and more. We submit ourselves to You and we seek Your wisdom for the journey ahead. We give you all praise and glory for all that You have done and what You will do. Please, Lord, hide Your Words in our hearts and bring them to our remembrance as we seek to win souls for Your kingdom. We are fully depending on You and not ourselves. We love You, Lord, and thank You for loving us so much that You sent Your only begotten Son to die for our sins. Please forgive us for every sin, in thought, word, deed, and omission. We turn away from the darkness of our past and seek the light found in You. In Jesus' name, we pray. Amen.

FOR DISCUSSION

Chapter 8

1. Did you find viewing the Bible by sections helpful to you?

2. Do you feel that the Old Testament is no longer relevant? Why?

3. What is the difference between knowledge and wisdom?

4. Do we ever get to the point that we know all of God's Word?

5. What can a new convert offer for the mission we are all called to accomplish?

6. Are you struggling to study the entire Bible? If so, have you utilized different translations to find one that may be easier for you to read than the King James Version?

7. Have you considered reading through the Bible with family members or another

group?

Do You Hear Him Calling?

Chapter 9

The Emanuel 9:

June 17, 2015

Pastor Clementa Pinckney (39)

Reverend Daniel Simmons (79)

Reverend Sharonda Singleton (45)

Reverend DePayne Middleton (59)

Minister Myra Thompson (59)

Tywanza Sanders (26),

Cynthia Hurd (54),

Ethel Lance (70)

Susie Jackson (87)

The Emanuel 12:

Includes the nine who lost their

lives and three survivors:
Felicia Sanders
Felicia's 11 year old
granddaughter
Polly Sheppard
Charleston, South Carolina

News reporter and cameraman
murdered on TV
August 26, 2015
Allison Parker (24)
Adam Ward (29)
Survivor: Vicki Gardner
Roanoke, Virginia

Each day, for greater than a month after the tragic murders that took place in a local church during Bible Study, residents of the state of South Carolina watched the nine names of the victims who died scroll on television screens, as our nation was stunned by what occurred. There was little mention of the three survivors, whose lives were forever changed, during that time.

A little more than two months later, the nation again sat stunned as we viewed tragedy play out during a live broadcast of the news. These kinds of terrible incidents have played out far too many times over the world. It is also tragic that we have repeatedly gone from stunned, to tears, to anger, to forgiveness, to determination to make a difference, then back to life as usual. We have stood by waiting for the next horrible thing to happen and have even come to expect the unimaginable to one day occur.

The year 2015 has been marked by countless acts of violence, with an increase in frequency. This is also the year when the United States made same sex unions legal, and, we are wrapping up the year with the politicians taking full advantage of every media outlet, to degrade each other, in hopes of one day holding the highest office in our nation.

It is imperative that we pause to examine the condition of this world during the time that we live. It is no longer acceptable that the people of God continue to just exist in a state of indecision, while the enemy is steadily making his presence known in countless ways. So, I want you to ask yourself, do your hear Him calling you, yet?

Nobody has the authority to tell someone else what God has called them to do or who He has called them to be, but anyone who knows the Word of God can and should point believers to His Word. ***John 10: 2-10*** says, ***But he that entereth in by the door is the shepherd of*** *the sheep. To him the porter openeth; and the sheep hear his voice: and he calleth his own sheep by name, and leadeth them out. And when he putteth forth his own sheep, he goeth before them, and the sheep follow him: for they know his voice. And a stranger they will not follow, but will flee from him: for they know not the voice of strangers. This parable spake Jesus unto them: but they understood not what things they were which he spake unto them. Then said Jesus unto them again, Verily, verily, I say unto you, I am the door of the sheep. All that ever came before me are thieves and robbers: but the sheep did not hear them. I am the door: by me if any man enter in, he shall be saved, and shall go in and out, and find pasture. The thief cometh not, but for to steal, and to kill, and to destroy: I am come that they might have life, and that they might have it more abundantly...*

What is notable about this parable

Jesus spoke is that many quote that last verse about abundant life, but when read within the context of the parable, we can see that He is speaking of the sheep living abundantly, because they are following the Shepherd's leading voice. He says that once we hear His voice and follow Him, we shall go in and out and find pasture. Pasture, for sheep, is sustenance. What I see in this parable is that if any Christian is unsure of the voice of God leading them into service, they can "***go in and out, and find pasture***". Anyone that is not hearing Jesus' call on their life must be concerned and moved to action. Now, you must see that having entered in (accepted salvation), you now have the benefit of access to The Lord for direction. This is too important to be ignored.

Let us look closely at the whole of the parable. First, this reality of hearing the voice of Our Lord, to know what He has called us to do, begins with salvation. So we must begin by addressing those who are not yet saved. ***Verse 9*** begins by saying ***I am the door: by me if any man enter in, he shall be saved ...*** So Jesus identifies Himself as The Door and states this prerequisite for becoming His sheep.

Romans 10:9 says, ***That if thou shalt confess with thy mouth the Lord Jesus, and shalt believe in thine heart that God hath raised him from the dead, thou shalt be saved.***

This verse is so clear in explaining that if you know and believe that Jesus is Lord and that God raised Him from the dead, then confess what you believe verbally, and right now, you can be saved. If you have just accepted Jesus as Lord of your life, then take this moment to pray this prayer.

> *Dear Lord, please forgive me for all of my sins. Wash me from the inside to the outside, as I live the rest of my life for Your Glory. Thank You for*

making me sure, in my heart that Your Son, Jesus, is Lord, that He died to pay for my sins on Calvary's cross, and that You raised Him from the dead. I accept Your Word that tells me that I hear Your voice and will hear You, as You lead me on my life's journey. Speak to my heart and lead me, in Jesus' name. Amen.

You are now a member of the body of Christ. Continue to pray and ask God to lead you to a church where His Word is being taught, proclaimed, and lived.

Next, let us address those who are saved, but are not sure that they are hearing from The Lord. The Word of God is true and this means that you are indeed hearing His voice. There are many things in life that may cause a believer the uncertainty you are going through. There may be others in your life who you are listening to or walking so closely with that you have placed too much trust in man, and therefore man's voice has drowned out God's voice. There may be sin in your life that you have been unwilling to turn away from, and that sin may drown His voice out. You may be among Christians who are not confessing the scripture, found in **John 10.**

As addressed in a previous chapter, we are living in a time in which many are choosing what they will believe within the Word and what they will eliminate from their belief. So the whole of God's Word is not being proclaimed nor taught. So today, you need to engage in self examination and purpose that you will accept the whole of God's Word, because He is speaking to you. It is not possible for me to list everything that may be at work in your life to keep you from knowing His voice, but if you are uncertain, the need for self examination applies to you. **John 10:9** says that as a believer, you may enter in. The ways to enter in are through prayer, through The Word, and through meditation on The Word. Praying is a combination of speaking to God and hearing from Him, so speak to Him sincerely and let Him know that you need the assurance that He is speaking to you, and then wait on The Lord. Continue to go to Him, because He will reward those who diligently seek Him. You must be willing to obey Him, though, so if He is telling you let go of something you are holding on to, that is not good in your life, and whatever it is has become more valuable to you than your relationship with Him, then you already know why you are not hearing His voice. Do not wait to hear an audible voice. He is not a man, so He is not limited to the way that man speaks. He is Spirit, so He is unlimited. I do not suggest that it is impossible to hear Him audibly, because He is able to do all things, and there are some believers who profess to have heard an audible voice. I do not doubt them one bit, because I know He can do all things but fail. But I am saying that if you do not hear Him audibly, that does not mean that you are not hearing Him. You have His Spirit dwelling within You and the Spirit will confirm it for you, when you hear Him speaking to you. You have freedom to enter in, and seek what you need for the mission of God. Seek Him and He will give you life more abundantly. That is a benefit of salvation.

As tragedy after tragedy continues to plummet this world into deeper sin, the people who are called children of The Most High God need to rise up and become who God said we would be. All the way back in *Genesis*, God commanded that we have authority in this earth. He declared that *Death and life are in the power of the tongue: and they that love it shall eat the fruit thereof. Proverbs 18:21.*

We are not to sit back as there are mass shootings in movie theaters and at malls across this nation and wait for someone else to speak peace. We cannot walk by or drive pass, on our way to church, as more and more people are living on our nation's streets and eating from area trash receptacles.

It is an injustice that we drive daily over bridges, where others are living and sleeping under them. We must not be satisfied with singing the sweet songs of praise on Sundays, while we are not reading and believing the Word that we are singing about. The death of God's people across this nation was not in vain!

The hurt, pain, and confusion of the survivors of these tragedies is not to be forgotten or never acknowledged. What they are going through is not without a reason. We saw it and we lived through it, because God is trying to tell us something. We need to hear Him tell us, through the mass shootings, that we can't put off getting in His Word for a later time, because we may not be here at a later time. Hear Him telling us that we can't put off getting to know Him intimately because we may not have the words to say to a survivor, to help them to hold on to His unchanging hands, when everything they believed seems not to have helped them when they needed it most. We may not know how to let His light of comfort and care shine through us, when we are needed. We need to hear Him telling us that now is the day of salvation, through the death of the reporter and cameraman on live TV.

In the aftermath of the Emanuel 12 or the shooting on live TV, if you had the opportunity to speak with any of the survivors, would you know what to say or do, whereby God could use you to help them find their way to answers they are seeking from God, when man really has no answers?

Do you hear Him calling? Or are you waiting for an audible voice? Many of us are praying for Him to come back, in a super-natural way, and straighten out the mess that we have allowed to become the norm in the earth. But The Word is very clear about how He is going to return. No, this is not a fire and brimstone Word. This is a now Word. We were not here to do the things that Moses did during his time on the earth. We were not here to do David's job of leading the masses to victory after victory. We can't claim the victories of the many souls Paul won for the Master, during his day. But what are we doing for the Lord now, during our short time on this side? God spoke to those men in the Bible audibly, through angels, through other men, through inanimate objects even. His Word says He speaks to us and I know that His Word is true!

I call into bondage every demonic spirit

that keeps God's people from assurance that they are hearing from The Lord. And I loose every warring angel of God to battle for you who are reading this today, in the name of Jesus! I speak life into your Spirit and not death. I speak purpose of God into you right now, and as I type I pray for break-through for you. I cast out every spirit of confusion, defeat and fear in your life. I speak prosperity in your Spirit walk. I speak Godly wisdom in your soul. I speak financial blessings for the purpose of ministry and for your personal life, according to the Word of God which declares

"Beloved, I wish above all things that thou mayest prosper and be in health, even as thy soul prosperth..." 3 John 1:2.

I say Hallelujah, My Lord, for what You have spoken into the lives of Your people. Hallelujah, for what You are doing right

now, through Your Word You have sent forth to all You have chosen to read this book. I bless Your Holy Name, as I wait with expectation to see people accepting You as Lord and Savior in great numbers. I lift up Jesus' name, as I expect an abundance of believers who are working for Your Kingdom and no longer sitting down in complacency. I claim it and declare that it is done. In Jesus' name. Amen.

John 11:35-44

35 Jesus wept.

36 Then said the Jews, Behold how he loved him!

37 And some of them said, Could not this man, which opened the eyes of the blind, have caused that even this man should not have died?

38 Jesus therefore again groaning in himself cometh to the grave. It was a cave, and a stone lay upon it.

39 Jesus said, Take ye away the stone. Martha,

the sister of him that was dead, saith unto him, Lord, by this time he stinketh: for he hath been dead four days.

40 Jesus saith unto her, Said I not unto thee, that, if thou wouldest believe, thou shouldest see the glory of God?

41 Then they took away the stone from the place where the dead was laid. And Jesus lifted up his eyes, and said, Father, I thank thee that thou hast heard me.

42 And I knew that thou hearest me always: but because of the people which stand by I said it, that they may believe that thou hast sent me.

43 And when he thus had spoken, he cried with a loud voice, Lazarus, come forth.

44 And he that was dead came forth, bound hand and foot with graveclothes: and his face was bound about with a napkin. Jesus saith unto them, Loose him, and let him go.

There are four things I will bring your attention to, from this passage of scripture.

1. ***Jesus wept- 35***
2. ***Jesus prayed- 41-42***
3. ***Jesus spoke life into that which was dead- 43***
4. ***The dead came back to life- 44***

Jesus gives us a great and powerful pattern for following Him, in these verses. When we have wept over the dead, which could be physical death, the death of of hope and dreams, the death of your community, the death of your state or nation, the death of your health, your wealth, your family unit, your church, your whatever, it is time to stop weeping.

The emotional impact of the tragedies should end, because it is time to pray. So you pray and fast, fast and pray, then pray and fast some more. But out of praying and fasting "entering in", comes sustenance and strength to take action. Next, speak live into that thing, where death has settled so long until the stench of it has risen up all around it. And I declare, The Word declares, that the dead in Christ shall rise! Oh yes, there will be a resurrection morning, just as Mary and Martha thought that Jesus was talking about. But that coming resurrection is not the only resurrection. Jesus did not breathe new life into us for us to just wait for that eternal life one day. There is the authority to for us to breathe new life into dead things right here and right now, while we are yet alive to walk in obedience to The Word of God.

Everyone was not called to be a preacher, but if you were, then stop running, stop making excuses, accept your calling, and preach. Preaching is what Jesus does through the vessel of a human being. Preacher, however, has become little more than a title that modern man believes they have the authority to bestow on whom *they* choose. OH, they have challenged the authority of God, on a whole different level, in the 21st century.

The more progressive churches have established a whole set of rules that require those who are called submit themselves to man and to organizations in order to be allowed to preach. But accept the call of

God on your life, if He has called you, because whom God calls, He will use. God has all authority and a called preacher preaches. That's what he does. Everyone wasn't called for administration. We are not all blessed with administrative skills, but if that is what you were called to do, then accept the call on your life. And allow God to make you the best administrator this world has ever seen.

We were not all called to be a teacher, but if you were, then equip yourself to walk in your calling. Answer your call with a resounding, "Yes, Lord!". Allow God to teach you so that you may teach others. There are some preachers who were also called to be teachers. All preachers teach also, through the preached Word, but not all were called to work in the position of a teacher. Will you accept your call to teach today?

I cannot even imagine all that God may call His people to do, for His Kingdom, but this one thing I do know, and that is, He is calling His people to service. The challenge today is for us to get serious about the things of God. All four Gospels proclaim that we must lay down our lives for The Lord.

1. Matthew 16:25 For whosoever will save his life shall lose it: whosoever will lose his life for my sake shall find it.

2. Mark 8:35 For whosoever will save his life shall lose it; but whosoever shall lose his life for my sake and the gospel's, the same shall save it.

3. Luke 9:24 For whosoever will save his life shall lose it: but whosoever will lose his life for my sake, the same shall save it.

4. John 12:25 He that loveth his life shall lose it; and he that hateth his life in this world shall keep it unto life eternal.

So what is it that you find yourself compelled to give up your way of life for? Are you willing to give it up, in order to obey God's calling?

Many people are more than willing to send money to help various charities, but some are not so willing to spend quality time in prayer. Many are willing to get involved in causes that will bring notoriety to their name, but are not as willing to work from the back seat to help where it is so badly needed. Sometimes we are willing to spend time in prayer, but are not willing to go out and visit someone who may need to see our face or hear our voice. There is absolutely nothing wrong with sending money to fund God's work, spending time in prayer for others who are on the front lines, working from the background, or visiting those who are going through. The evaluation is, are you willing to do *either* of these things, if you know that you have heard from The Lord?

Here, in the Charleston, South Carolina area, there is a mission organization called the **Charleston Area Justice Ministry**. It is a network of congregations who have come together to make Charleston a more just place to live. They have made a difference in our school system, in our court system, and most recently, in fair wages for employees. I have not joined their effort personally, as that is not where I have been lead, but my church has recently become a part of their efforts, and this ministry has proven very effective in our county. I am certain that there are other ministries with similar missions, where you live.

If not, you may visit their website, www.charlestonareajusticeministry.org and see how their group was organized and what they have accomplished. It may help to give you some direction in helping others. Then seek information in your area, where you may join efforts for justice. Pray for God to lead you, and be ready to follow.

The two previous chapters motivated us to get in The Word and to receive the whole of God's Word, and I was certainly encouraged to spend some more time in the Old Testament. We have spent most of this chapter in the Gospels, but we are about to go into the Old Testament to take a look at the repercussions of stepping out without hearing from God and/or stepping out ahead of Him, during ministry. We have all been motivated and inspired, and now we want to make certain that we stay behind the cross, as we step out in ministry. We really don't want our flesh to get in the way of God's glory. Come and go with me to ***1 Chronicles 13: 5-12 and 1 Chronicles 21.***

> 5 So David gathered all Israel together, from Shihor of Egypt even unto the entering of Hemath, to bring the ark of God from Kirjathjearim.
>
> 6 And David went up, and all Israel, to Baalah, that is, to Kirjathjearim, which belonged to Judah, to bring up thence the ark of God the Lord, that dwelleth between the cherubims, whose name is called on it.

7 And they carried the ark of God in a new cart out of the house of Abinadab: and Uzza and Ahio drave the cart.

8 And David and all Israel played before God with all their might, and with singing, and with harps, and with psalteries, and with timbrels, and with cymbals, and with trumpets.

9 And when they came unto the threshingfloor of Chidon, Uzza put forth his hand to hold the ark; for the oxen stumbled.

10 And the anger of the Lord was kindled against Uzza, and he smote him, because he put his hand to the ark: and there he died before God.

11 And David was displeased, because the Lord had made a breach upon Uzza: wherefore that place is called Perezuzza to this day.

12 And David was afraid of God that day, saying, How shall I bring the ark of God home to me?

We find that David, who was described as a man after God's own heart, has become known as a great leader and warrior. God Himself has added numerous followers for David to lead. Repeatedly, throughout ***1 Chronicles***, David receives detailed instructions from God for leading God's people. And he gives out the commands to the people. He told them who would serve in various positions of service to God. He gave (relayed) the orders, to include who would be the singers, the directors, and who would be anointed to carry the ark of the covenant, as the Israelites moved from place to place. We find, in the text from ***1 Chronicles 13: 5-12***, that David and the people are praising God with instruments and singing, as the ark represented the presence of The Lord with them. But the oxen pulling the cart that was carrying the ark stumbled and someone who was not anointed to touch the ark, reached out his hand to hold the ark, and this kindled the anger of God. God smote him and he died right there and then. David is described in the text as first, displeased with what God had done, and then, as afraid of God. Note the question that he then poses. ***How shall I bring the ark of God home to me?*** David notes that something had gone wrong, which was a breach. This means that, having walked closely with God, in obedience, he was assured by God that it was time to bring the ark back home to the Israelites: but the Lord, having smote one of the Israelites, was clearly stating that He was addressing a problem with them. And now, David does not know how to proceed from that point.

This text provides a scenario that we often find in lives of service to Our Lord. So, as I begin to move toward the end of this book, I refer you back to chapter one, **Someone is Calling Me to Get Back in the Saddle Again.** Do you remember, ***1 Samuel 16: 13 Then Samuel took the horn of oil, and anointed him in the midst of his brethren: and the Spirit of the Lord came upon David from that day forward. So Samuel rose up, and went to Ramah.***

We know that David was anointed. We know that he was called to do the work he is doing in *1 Chronicles*, but something has gone horribly wrong on this day. The text cries out that what we do in service must remain in God's sovereign order; God first, God's chosen, anointed servants next.

1 Corinthians 12:24-25 For our comely parts have no need: but God hath tempered the body together, having given more abundant honour to that part which lacked. That there should be no schism in the body; but that the members should have the same care one for another. We must never place ourselves in the place of God and we must never step out first and hope that God is pleased. That is not God's order. This passage of scripture, states who is in charge, God. Then the body is tempered together by Him and each member should have the same care for one another. This means that, without regard to what each member is called to do, all are equal within the body. God has much to say to us, so that we may obey His command, and for this reason, we must seek Him for our calling and throughout our service to Him, or there undoubtedly will be a breach.

Read ***1 Chronicles 22.*** Again, David is tempted by Satan, this time, to count the number of the armies of Israel. Note that God did not tell David to count anyone. It is most notable that, when tempted by Satan, God provided Joab to speak with David. Joab told David the truth. It was God who increased the size of your followers, not you. We see, when God enlarges our coast, we must always remember that it is God who has done a great work, not we ourselves. But in ***chapter 22***, we find that David pulls rank on Joab and demands that he, the king, is obeyed. God is not pleased with David and sends David's seer, Gad, to present him with three choices for punishment. Note that God is not speaking to David directly here. There has been a breach.

Are you wondering why you may not be hearing God who is speaking to you? Well, maybe you have become full of self, like David was in this case. Continue to read the chapter and find that eventually, God does allow David to build another altar to Him, when David lines back up with the realization that He can do nothing without God. The owner of the threshing-floor, where David builds the altar, offers to give David everything he needed to build the altar and even the oxen for the burnt offering. But David paid full price for everything, realizing that he can't take from someone else to make an offering to The Lord. He has to earn what he is offering, in this case, pay for what he would offer unto God. Why would Ornan, the owner of the threshing-floor, make the sacrifice in David's stead? David was a man after God's own heart. He made the trespass and he was responsible for making it right with God. ***1 Chronicles 21: 30*** explains that even after The Lord received the burnt offering at the altar David made, David was still unable to approach the tabernacle of The Lord, which he had built in the wilderness and the altar of the burnt offering that were in Gibeon, because he remained afraid of the angel of The Lord who had risen up against them in punishment for having numbered the troops. He learned how to wait on The Lord.

Do you hear God calling you? The death of God's people recently, in America and other places around the world, were not in vain. The hurt, pain, and confusion of the survivors is not unnoticed or forgotten. The struggles of people around the world are not in vain. The troubles in our homes, churches, jobs, and communities are not to be taken lightly. God is loudly and clearly trying to tell us something. He is not telling any of us to go forward to address any of the concerns, without direction from Him. He is telling us that He has made Himself available to us. He is calling you to enter in. Get into The Word. Enter in, through fasting and prayer. Enter in, through surrender and meditation. Listen for the call of God on your life, accept His call, and prepare yourself for greater service to Our Lord, because the whole earth is groaning for The Savior. What is your role in God's perfect plan to take His people from Revelation back to Genesis? **Do you hear God calling you? 1 Chronicles 29-10-13**

10 Wherefore David blessed the Lord before all the congregation: and David said, Blessed be thou, Lord God of Israel our father, for ever and ever.

11 Thine, O Lord is the greatness, and the power, and the glory, and the victory, and the majesty: for all that is in the heaven and in the earth is thine; thine is the kingdom, O Lord, and thou art exalted as head above all.

12 Both riches and honour come of thee, and thou reignest over all; and in thine hand is power and might; and in thine hand it is to make great, and to give strength unto all.

13 Now therefore, our God, we thank thee, and praise thy glorious name.

This chapter is dedicated to the Survivors of the 2015 tragedy at Emanuel AME Church in Charleston, South Carolina

Survivors, you may not fully understand God's will and direction for your life right now, and I would never say that I understand it at all. But there is one thing, I do know. Our God is nearer to you than the skin that covers you, and He does have a reason that you are still here. You certainly may need the strength of others right now, but just hold on and never give up on God, because in time, others will be getting their strength from you. One reason that you were spared is very clear to me. That is, because He found you to be strong enough to be used by Him, after all that you went through and are still going through. Continue to enter in through prayer and fasting and He will answer your questions.

Exactly how He plans to use you, He will reveal to you, in His perfect time, and I pray that I am alive to see you shine.

We say, hallelujah to You, Our Lord! And our souls say yes, to Your will.

FOR DISCUSSION

Chapter 9

1. Have you been moved to action, based on emotions instead of hearing from God?

2. Do you recognize God speaking to your Spirit, through others?

3. Are you walking closely with The Lord today? If not, did you find directions for drawing closer to Him?

4. Even though this chapter did not include a written sermon, did you recommit yourself during the call to salvation?

5. Did you find the need for self-examination to address the issues in your life that may be affecting how clearly you are hearing from God?

6. Have you ever invited someone to come to Christ? Do you feel empowered to do

so?

7. In the text taken from ***John 11:35-44*** we saw that Jesus wept over the death of Lazarus. Have you wept over the condition of our world? Are you encouraged to move from weeping into prayer and action, through God's Word?

8. What do you think of when you hear the term "enter in" within the Word?

9. Are you willing to give up something in your life, that God has been dealing with you concerning, in order to draw nearer to God?

10. Will you go forward, with a keener awareness of the divine order of God in your life and service?

____

____

____

____

Work for the Night is Coming

Chapter 10

I have said very little about myself throughout this book, other than sharing my personal experience concerning what motivated me to get started writing the book, and later, my confession as a former disgruntled employee. The entire writing was to motivate you to focus or re-focus on your calling. There is no reason to elevate myself, because I can save no-one. I do not have the power and authority to call anyone to be anything. And, I certainly do not have the ability to sustain anyone.

David could no more have saved Uzza's life, when the wrath of God was displayed, than I could if He rose against someone in my life. Therefore, I point no spot-light on myself. Instead, I have spent more than twenty years proclaiming primarily two messages. They have been, "put your trust in God and not in man", and "united we will stand, divided we will surely fall". I have attacked, unashamedly, every device of the enemy, and his every attempt to divide and conquer the people of God. I have boldly asserted that no man has authority over God. Choose God, through Jesus, over man all the time! Now, God has added "get up and work for The Lord, people of God", as a message for me to spread to His people.

Just as in the chapter entitled **Taking it from Genesis to Revelation**, I will refer back to the beginning of this book, to bring your attention to another point that is revealed, and in doing so, I will also share something more about myself. Beginning with chapter one, the book reveals that God started this writing long before that Saturday morning that I got up and began to organize these ten chapters. Many of the sermons that were included had already been written and preached, but at the time, I did not realize that they would also appear in a book. I am directing your attention to the obvious, for a reason. What God is calling you to do has already begun. God is a Spirit. Man was created in His image. Your calling is already existing, in the Spirit realm, before it is manifested in the natural. It is activated, in the natural, when you step out on faith.

This chapter was titled after a sermon I preached for the first time in 2013, which you will read later, but before you get into it, let me share a very personal experience with you, because I believe it will help someone who may be struggling to step out on faith. In chapter one, I gave instructions concerning the need to do things in proper order. I said, confide in your spiritual leader. Years ago, when I finally accepted the call on my life to preach, I found myself in such a state of apprehension, that I had taken a week off from work. God had already given me so many sermons, which I had refused to write down, until I was full to nearly bursting. So, from the sermons within me, I began to write motivational "speeches" and "words of encouragement", but I refused to call any of them sermons. I was determined not to become a preacher, at that time. From there, I commenced to writing a business plan, in order to promote myself, so that I could seek opportunities to **motivate people to choose and to follow Jesus.** Upon completion of this rough draft of my intent, the Spirit told me to go and speak with my Pastor concerning what I was doing, before I took another step.

I called the Pastor, and he said for me to come to the church. I know that we met for about two hours or longer. I explained my plans and sought his prayers and support. I explained, during the conversation, how I had all of this within me for a long time, but had never written it down. I told him of my fear that if I didn't get started I may forget some of what God had already given me and, in fact, thought that I possibly had already forgotten some of it. My Pastor simply asked me why I had never written any of what God gave me down. He was very good at listening. His question set me to rambling on some more. I immediately began to protest and confess that I do not want to be a preacher. I told him, in no uncertain terms, that I would not become a part of what I had observed over the years, so I refused to write anything down. Please note that my Pastor never said a word to me about preaching. But what he did do was allow me the freedom to confess what was inside of me. And what he said next (after I was completely done with my presentation) was exactly what I needed to hear. He said, "God did not call you to conform to what you have observed in this world. You are what we call, in Psychology, a non-conformist. Let's pray." He held my hand, and as I shed a few tears, my Pastor prayed for me.

Three weeks later, after he never said another word to me about our visit, I went back to him and told him I had accepted the call on my life to preach the Gospel.

Long before manifestation in the natural, your calling is already existing in the Spirit realm. Do not be ashamed to share what God has given you, with your spiritual leader. That person will surely pray with and for you. That day, my Pastor was told that I would preach, write, and motivate others for My Lord. It is with humility and thanksgiving that I write these words. My Pastor was used in a mighty way in my life. So I give all praise, honor, and glory to my Savior, Jesus, followed by a sincere tribute to my Pastor, in divine order. Please note that I have intentionally left his name out of this book, but with his permission, I will include his name on all personally signed copies. I will also include his name in my second publication, with his permission, so stay tuned for the next published work!

Now, come and go with me, into the final sermon:

Work for the Night is Coming

2 Corinthians 4:1-11

1 Therefore seeing we have this ministry, as we have received mercy, we faint not;

2 But have renounced the hidden things of dishonesty, not walking in craftiness, nor handling the word of God deceitfully; but by manifestation of the truth commending ourselves to every man's conscience in the sight of God.

3 But if our gospel be hid, it is hid to them that are lost:

4 In whom the god of this world hath blinded the minds of them which believe not, lest the light of the glorious gospel of Christ, who is the image of God, should shine unto them.

5 For we preach not ourselves, but Christ Jesus the Lord; and ourselves your servants for Jesus' sake.

6 For God, who commanded the light to shine out of darkness, hath shined in our hearts, to give the light of the knowledge of the glory of God in the face of Jesus Christ.

7 But we have this treasure in earthen vessels, that the excellency of the power may be of God, and not of us.

8 We are troubled on every side, yet not distressed; we are perplexed, but not in despair;

9 Persecuted, but not forsaken; cast down, but not destroyed;

10 Always bearing about in the body the dying of the Lord Jesus, that the life also of Jesus might be made manifest in our body.

11 For we which live are always delivered unto death for Jesus' sake, that the life also of Jesus might be made manifest in our mortal flesh...

Introduction: The message is that we must work, throughout every situation we face. We must not allow any circumstance, to include the fact that God is still working on us, to stop us from pressing forward on the mission we are to accomplish.

1. As we ponder the verses given for the

message, we must first consider what is meant by the word work, and specifically for the church, what is meant by mission work. Verse 1 states that we have received this ministry. This applies to the mission assignment given to us.

2. We will look at what service looks like for the Church, as Paul has described in verse 2. It is imperative that, as we go about the Father's business, we hold true to the three characteristics of Christian service, as given in the Word of God.

3. We must consider the challenges that would hinder or stop the Church while on our mission. Paul identifies many things that would cause some to faint, in verses 8-11. We will look at how these verses come to life in the believer's walk.

This message is a wake up call for the body of Christ. As we compare what the church looked like in the days of the Bible to what we look like today, we find that the present day church has become more and more prideful and slothful. It has been deceived into believing that we must sound good, look good and feel good. It appears that we also believe that in working for the Lord, the end justifies the means by which we reach it. In fact, the Word teaches that, in the Lord's service, these things are not true. Work that is devoid of the precepts, statutes and concepts of our Lord is not really Christian service at all. The sad commentary is that often times the church is going about its own business and not The Lord's business. The only way for us to get on course and stay on course is to run to the Word for correction and direction for ourselves. This is vitally important, because indeed the Word advises us repeatedly that in the last days, there would be perilous times and that many would be deceived. So let us allow Him to address some of these deceptions, by considering the Word.

First, let us begin in ***Matthew*** and evaluate what the mission of the church is. ***Matthew 28:19*** tells the church to Go ye therefore and teach all nations. The Word further tells us to Work out our own salvation with fear and trembling ***Philippians 2:12***. He says to become fishers of men ***Matthew 4:19***, which means winning souls for the Master. ***Acts 1:8*** says that the believers will receive power, after the Holy Ghost is come, to go throughout the world and be witnesses for Jesus. These scriptures identify what the mission of the church was and still is today. Simply stated, we are commanded to work. ***2 Corinthians 4:2*** gives us a little insight into "how" we are to do the work, ***But have renounced the hidden things of dishonesty, not walking in craftiness, nor handling the word of God deceitfully; but by manifestation of the truth commending*** *ourselves to every man's conscience in the sight of God..*

<u>Point 1</u>

We go all the way back to ***Genesis*** to find where work for mankind first started. We recall that after God created man in His image, in chapter 3 man sins. After this act of disobedience to God, we find that He gave out three curses upon His creation. Unto the serpent, God said in

Genesis 3: 14 And the Lord God said unto the serpent, Because thou hast done this, thou art cursed above all cattle; and above every beast of the field; upon thy belly shalt thou go, and dust shalt thou eat all the days of thy life. To this day, I have not seen a snake any other way than slithering to and fro.

Genesis 3: 16 Unto the woman He said, I will greatly multiply thy sorrow and thy conception; in sorrow thou shall bring forth children; and thy desire shall be to thy husband; and he shall rule over thee.

Some of us think that just because some wise person created good anesthesia, and epidurals make it seem so much easier than it once was to give birth, we are getting by without the pain and suffering. But I'm here to point out the many nights, when the little ones are giving us both pain and sorrow, many men are able to sleep, because God's Word must be fulfilled. What we are focusing on today is..

Genesis 3:17 And unto Adam he said, Because thou hast hearkened unto the voice of thy wife, and hast eaten of the tree, of which I commanded thee saying Thou shalt not eat of it: cursed is the ground for thy sake; in sorrow shalt thou eat of it all the days of thy life. 3:19 In the sweat of thy face shalt thou eat bread, till thou return unto the ground; for out of it wast thou taken: for dust thou art, and unto dust shalt thou return.

Working does go way back. Noah had a whole lot of work to do and not a lot of help. We find that the Israelites, God's chosen people, were enslaved and made to work hard under harsh task-masters. Then they went from assignment to assignment, in wars to capture lands wherever God lead them. We find that the prophets had to work, and traveled miles to do so. The disciples and apostles worked hard, in the midst of threats and rejection. Jesus had to work hard, in order to fulfill the Word. So, what about you and me? Modern day Christianity is leading people to believe that the nicer we look and the more possessions we have, the more closely we are walking with The Lord. We have moved away from "cleanliness (inside an outside) is next to godliness". We have bought into the concept that we must all get dressed up in our finest, keep the fingernails done, the hair perfected, drive the finest vehicles, and live in homes with all of the present day amenities, in Jesus' name, and we are representing Our

Lord. In actuality, we are sending mixed messages that are untrue. We fail in presenting the truth of salvation, in our desire to prove that we have arrived. If we look to the scriptures, for how we are to present ourselves, we find a different story. I don't believe we would find Noah dressed in his finest attire, but we'd find him sweaty, probably dirty and tired, but doing the work of The Lord. I don't believe we would find Paul sitting in private rooms, designed fashionably for the elite, to do God's work. We would find, in the Word, that Paul did most of his work from behind prison walls. He obeyed the call on his life, in spite of how he was living, where he was living, and how uncomfortable his surroundings may have been. It really is time for the church to get serious about what and who God has called us to be. Being about the Father's business and not our own requires hard work, and many times it doesn't look or feel very good. ***Mark 6: 7-9*** says, ***And he called unto him the twelve, and began to send them forth by two and two; and gave them power over unclean spirits; And command them that they should take nothing for their journey, save a staff only; no scrip, no bread, no money in their purse: But be shod with sandals; and not put on two coats.*** Wow! What a description of earthen vessels, called to do the work of God. We must remember ***2 Corinthians 4: 7 But we have this treasure in earthen vessels, that the excellency of the power may be of God, and not of us.***

<u>Point 2</u>

Let us turn our attention to what Paul is telling us in ***2 Corinthians 4: 1.*** Paul gives us warning that, as we are called to ministry, there would be reasons that we would faint, but he reminds us that the reason we do not faint is because we have received mercy. ***4: 2*** gives us the first insight into reasons the believer may have for fainting during ministry, if it were not for this mercy we have received. First, ***we have renounced the hidden things of dishonesty.*** Second, we are ***not walking in craftiness.*** And third, we are ***not handling the word of God deceitfully.*** These three facts all point to who we are in character, since we are born again believers in Christ. These are also the characteristics that must be present in every work to which we are called. They are also the characteristics that draw the attacks of the enemy. They differentiate God's work from the devil's work. Without them, we have only the "form of godliness". Notice how many negative terms Paul is using to describe what we are Not. The term renounced means that that we have not only turned away from these things that are not characteristic of believers, but in fact, we have totally rejected these hidden things of dishonesty. It doesn't simply mean that we don't practice the hidden dishonesty, the craftiness, and the use of God's Word deceitfully. It's a whole lot more than than just not being involved in these things and turning away from them. A renouncement is better defined with the boldness of declaration that, "these characteristics ***define*** what is evil, forbidden of the God we serve, and reprobate behavior that come straight from the devil". We reject the devil and all of his tactics are found to be repulsive. We turn to and embrace our God, godliness, holiness, faithfulness, and honesty, And We Are Bold About It, Unashamed, and Unapologetic!

See, Paul was a new man, when he was changed. He spoke the truth with honesty and boldness, and he didn't play footsies with those who were in opposition to the truth. The same way that he persecuted the church with zeal when he was in the world, he proclaimed the gospel with zeal. He didn't partake in crafty schemes to leave anyone questioning where he stood or what he believed. He did not handle the Word deceitfully, playing with and bending the truth to make anyone come on board without understanding what new life meant. He wasn't trying to appease others. When we stand firmly, without apology, on the truth of God's Word, we are on opposite ends of a rope, fully engaged in a tug of war. That is because we are new, and the light that shines through us cannot be put out by the darkness of this world.

The Word teaches us that the devil is a deceiver, he is crafty, and he is the father of lies. Look at ***Genesis 3: 1*** where Satan begins by asking the woman, ***Yea, hath God said, Ye shall not eat of every tree of the garden?*** That's how he starts out, with his craftiness. Who doesn't realize that this snake knew what he came to do when he approached Eve? See, deceitful, manipulative, dishonest people are thinking of the approach, what your response will be, how they will lead you in conversation, at what juncture they should pause for effect, and even when to lift an eyebrow to add expression. Paul is warning us to think before we leap, when we are out there in the real world representing Our Lord. And if we didn't learn anything from the snake in ***Genesis***, at least we need to take the warning that, when we see a snake, we are not to play with it. We are not to engage in a lot of unnecessary conversations. ***James 1: 19*** says, ***Wherefore, my beloved brethren, let every man be swift to hear, slow to speak, slow to wrath:*** We are to recognize the characteristics for what they are, and stay focused on the mission at hand. We are to renounce this evil. What I want us to really take away from this scripture is that this kind of bold rejection of dishonesty, craftiness and deceitfulness is reason enough to make the devil, and all those who have fallen prey to him, angry. The result of this anger is "the attack". Paul is letting the believer know that when we walk in this newness of life, we are to be ready for the attacks and STAND ANYWAY: we faint not, because we have also received mercy to stand and to endure, for the cause of Christ.

2 Corinthians 4: 2b goes on to say, ***but by manifestation of the truth, commending ourselves to every man's conscience in the sight of God.*** When we renounce the negative things of evil, we are not only wide open for the attacks, from outside and even within the body of Christ, but we also line our lives up for God's use and service to others. Part b of the verse confirms the fact that everyone who witnesses our lives have a conscience. Paul is drawing a clear line in the sand here and saying, *whose report will you believe?.* Are those who view God at work in our lives and hear us proclaim the power and glory of God able to deny the manifestation of His truth, and believe the deceiver? No, when they see our lives, it should be undeniable that God's Word is at work within us.

Point 3 Manifestation of the Truth

We are facing many challenges, so we must take encouragement from the Word and stand firm for Jesus. ***Verses 5-11*** shares the challenges Paul faced and we will also face in ministry. First, we are reaching out to non-believers whose minds are blinded by sin. In true ministry to God, we preach Jesus Christ the Lord; and ourselves, servants to the people, for Jesus' sake. And herein lies the problem, the devil doesn't want us to lift up the name of Jesus. He doesn't care a bit if we present ourselves as perfectly attired, success stories, as long as we are not lifting up Jesus' name. He didn't want Adam and Eve to obey God, all the way back in the garden, and he doesn't want us to obey Him today. He will always fight us in ministry.

We can easily see that the reason Paul has spent much time explaining this in Chapter 4 is because he was always going through attacks during his ministry. He knew what kept him and he knew what the believers would need in order to endure.

In **verse 7**, where he acknowledges us as earthen vessels, it is an acknowledgment of more than the fact that we are imperfect people. It affirms that, we are going to feel while we are going through, we are going to hurt going through, we are going to shed tears while going through the many trials, and sometimes we are going to fail miserably, because this treasure of the Spirit of God is within earthen vessels. And he clearly gives us the reason. It is not so that we may fail and be embarrassed in front of other earthen vessels. It's not so that the devil may have any power over our lives.

It is for the stated purpose that the whole world may see (believe and know) that the excellency: the victories, the strength and supernatural ability to endure in the face of threatening situations, disappointments and sometimes failure is of God.

It is not because we are so good, so smart, so educated, so successful, and oh so enviable. We succeed, endure, excel, and are victorious, because we are the living **manifestation of the Truth.** When Jesus lived here on the earth, He was The Word, incarnate; that's the Word come to life in flesh form. Now, we, as believers, must also represent that The Word is true, in flesh form. To God be the glory at all times! Great things He and He alone, has done!

Verse 8 says, ***We are troubled on every side*** (so is the world), but the verse says for us ***but not in distress.*** See, the world doesn't see God in us through the fact that we are troubled on every side. They have troubles too. They see God in the fact that ***we*** are not in distress during the trouble, like the world is. In fact, the Word says that we are to be steadfast and unmovable ***1 Corinthians 15:58.*** The Word says that we are like a tree that's planted by the rivers of water, ***Psalm 1:3.*** Church, that's what shows that the excellency is of God and not of ourselves. We are ***perplexed*** (so is the world), but for us it says, ***but not in despair.*** Yes, we are found wondering sometimes what our next step should be, just like everyone else, but we are not in despair, because we know, according to the Word, that when we call Him, He will answer. We don't know when and we don't even know how the answer is going to come, but we ***know*** that our Help is with us during these times. How we are going through proclaims Who is leading us. The Word says, ***Persecuted*** (just like the world), ***but not forsaken*** (just like a child of God), ***Cast down*** (like the world), ***but not destroyed*** (because we have this mercy). Understand and accept that the whole wide world is going to see us go through heart-ache and pain, if we stand boldly and renounce the hidden things of dishonesty, if we do not deal in craftiness nor handle the Word of God deceitfully. But we have got to be determined to work for The Lord anyway. In fact, we work even harder for Him, because He is making His presence known to us and through us. We work day and night for Him, because He is worthy.

Working for the Lord requires that we stay holy in His work. Stay righteous in His work. The holiness and righteousness, the "can't stop" attitude, the "refuse to stop" determination, the "will not compromise the Truth" focus, in the face of all obstacles and challenges, is what brings forth the manifestation of ***Whose*** we are and ***Who*** we are serving. The 21st century church must work untiringly on behalf of the Truth, because the Word tells us that in the last days there will be perilous times. Men will be lovers of themselves and lovers of pleasure more than lovers of God. This results in false teaching, false preaching, and confused minds. Many will be deceived, but the ecclesia (the called out ones) will stand and will work for the Lord. We thank God, today, that Paul has given us the warning, the tools, and the characteristics of work for Our Lord. And now I say, work! Work, for the night is coming.

If you have been called by God for service, then serve the Lord with your whole heart. If you have never given your life to God, then you must come in at the door. If you believe that Jesus is Lord, that He died for your sins and paid your sin-debt in full, and if you believe that God raised Jesus from the dead, then confess what you believe with your mouth. The Word says, thou shalt be saved. Pray and ask God to forgive you for your sins and receive you into His family. If you have made that awesome choice and have done this, you are a part of the body of Christ. Set your mind and your heart to get into the Word of God, and He will lead you to the work. God bless you.

FOR DISCUSSION

Chapter 10

1. Is there a difference between the mission of your church and your personal call? Discuss the differences and how they work together.

2. What gifts has God blessed you to use within your local congregation? What gifts are you using separate from your church affiliation?

3. Are you working as a part of a team or alone? If your answer is both, then discuss what challenges each bring to accomplishing tasks.

4. Do you regularly stop to evaluate your service and make sure that it has not strayed away from the precepts given in the Word?

5. Do you normally seek instructions from The Lord before you start on a

project or do you remember to seek Him after the project is started? Discuss how this affects what you set out to accomplish in ministry.

6. ***2 Corinthians 4: 8-10*** provides descriptive words for what Christians experience, when living for the Lord. Has any of them applied to an experience in your life? What helped you to endure during those times?

7. Are you walking closely with a spiritual leader in your life? This is not limited to your Pastor only, as there may be others in your life who serve in this capacity as well.

8. Do you write it down, when you receive revelation knowledge from The Lord? Why or why not?

9. Have you ever spoken with someone who is not saved about giving their life to Jesus? Can you readily find appropriate scriptures that will help you to do so?

10. Will you make the commitment to seek continually God's will for your life? Will you obey His call?

A Closing Word

Accepting Jesus as Lord of your life is the most important choice you will ever make. He has already chosen you, but He has left that final choice of salvation in your hands. If we did not have the freedom to choose, we would be like the precious animals that were created. We are the only ones into whom God blew the breath of life, and that is how we became a living soul. Since the fall of man, repentance has been and will always be the beginning of healing that breach which separated man from God, through sin.

We find, throughout the Old Testament, that the message of the prophets was repent, repent, repent. See *Ezekiel 18: 30 Therefore I will judge you, O house of Israel, every one according to his ways, saith the Lord God. Repent, and turn yourselves from all your transgressions; so iniquity shall not be your*

ruin. Then, in the New Testament, we find repent and be baptized. See ***Acts 2: 38 Then Peter said unto them, Repent, and be baptized every one of you in the name of Jesus Christ for the remission of sins, and ye shall receive the gift of the Holy Ghost.*** The call to repentance is consistent throughout the whole Word.

Repentance is vitally important, because it begins with admitting to yourself that you are wrong, admitting that you are sincerely sorry, and turning away from sin. This act of repentance does not mean that you will never sin again for the rest of your life. It means that you accept responsibility for your sin, and you have consciously chosen to turn away from sin and toward God. You see, Jesus died for your past, present, and future sins. To more clearly understand this fact, just remember that Jesus died for our sins more than two thousand years ago, before we were even born. When you are born again and you do sin, and you repent and ask Him to forgive you, He will forgive you. See ***1 John 1: 9 If we confess our sins, he is faithful and just to forgive us our sins, and to cleanse us from all unrighteousness.*** This means that He allows us back into right standing before God. This is because He loves us, and has paid for all of our sins.

Repentance is so very important, because it is your first act of surrendering to God. It symbolizes that you have chosen to stop fighting against Him, in your heart. We can't hear Him clearly, unless we surrender to Him. We can't obey Him fully, unless we surrender our will to His will. Repentance is just that vital to your walk with The Lord and mine.

I have been saved for more than forty years, and when I surrendered, I did not fully understand how repentance works. I knew, beyond the shadow of doubt, that Jesus was Lord. I knew, as a young *person, that The Word was true. I knew that when I asked God to forgive my sins, I was forgiven. I truly accepted that Jesus died for my sins and that God raised Him from the dead. I believed that Jesus was taking care of me. As a child, I was anxious to get up and tell my Pastor what I believed, when he extended the invitation to salvation.*

Please do not put off for tomorrow what you can do right now. Before you can accept the call of God on your life, you must accept Jesus as Lord. So pray and ask God to forgive you for your sins. Confess with your mouth that you believe that God has raised Jesus from the dead. Ask God to receive you as a member of His family, based upon the fact that Jesus paid for your sin, by the shedding of His blood. Thank Jesus for what He did and thank God for saving you. Finally, see

Romans 10: 10 For with the heart man believeth unto righteousness; and with the mouth confession is made unto salvation.

About the Author

Minister Robin Godfrey Bunkem is a woman of God who is not ashamed of the Gospel. She is a native of Charleston, South Carolina. She accepted salvation at the age of 10, and became a member of Calvary Baptist Church, in Charleston.

She began to minister to children who would share their stories of neglect and sometimes abuse with her, while she was still an elementary school student.

Minister Bunkem's life joy has always been sharing the truth of the Word. She is better known for singing the Lord's praises. She served as a member of several gospel choirs over a forty year period of time, and directed two youth choirs for twenty years.

Minister Bunkem accepted the call to the preaching ministry, preached her initial sermon in November of 2008, and became a licensed minister. She continues *to boldly deliver God's Word, whenever there is an opportunity.*

There are many scriptures on which her life and ministry is built, but the text that holds true through every experience in her life is ***Matthew 22: 36-40***, which commands that we first love our Lord and then our neighbors as ourselves. The personal belief that describes her character and drive is,

"Through the Word of God, we are developed to stand for what we believe, so that others are drawn to Christ through us. And in doing so, we will not fall for everything we see and hear in this world."

www.ingramcontent.com/pod-product-compliance
Lightning Source LLC
Chambersburg PA
CBHW051822040426
42447CB00006B/321

* 9 7 8 0 6 9 2 5 4 8 5 5 4 *